Unsubscribe

HOW TO KILL EMAIL ANXIETY,
AVOID DISTRACTIONS
AND GET REAL WORK DONE

JOCELYN K. GLEI

piatkus

PIATKUS

First published in the US in 2016 by Public Affairs, an imprint of Perseus Books, a division of PBG Publishing, LLC, a subsidiary of Hachette Book Group, Inc. First published in Great Britain in 2016 by Piatkus

Illustrations by Tomba Lobos

1 3 5 7 9 10 8 6 4 2

A CIP catalogue record for this book
is available from the British Library.

ISBN 978-0-349-41448-5

Printed and bound by CPI Group (UK) Ltd, Croydon, CR0 4YY

Papers used by Piatkus are from well-managed forests
and other responsible sources.

MIX
Paper from
responsible sources
FSC® C104740
www.fsc.org

Piatkus
An imprint of
Little, Brown Book Group
Carmelite House
50 Victoria Embankment
London EC4Y 0DZ

An Hachette UK Company
www.hachette.co.uk

www.improvementzone.co.uk

About the Author

Jocelyn K. Glei is a writer who's obsessed with how we can find more creativity and meaning in our daily work. She is the bestselling author and editor of three previous books that have sold over a quarter of a million copies: *Manage Your Day-to-Day*, *Maximize Your Potential*, and *Make Your Mark*, which offer pragmatic, actionable advice for creatives on managing their time, their careers, and their businesses. She was formerly the director of the 99U Conference and the founding editor of 99u.com, which earned two Webby awards for Best Cultural Blog and a rabid fan base of productivity nerds. She lives in Los Angeles and online at: jkglei.com.

About the Illustrator

Tomba Lobos is the illustration project of Portuguese artist José Cardoso. With a versatile style, Cardoso creates original artwork for both digital and print. He is always striving to push the limits of both his technique and his trademark aesthetic, a unique blend of the strange and humorous. Learn more about his work at: www.be.net /tombalobos.

EMAIL: A LOVE-HATE RELATIONSHIP

Email is broken. Or, more precisely, email has broken us. On a regular basis it inspires hatred, guilt, anxiety, anger, and despair. The very last thing we think about when we think about email is its utility. And yet we know it's a useful and necessary part of our everyday lives.

The true source of our love-hate relationship with email is that we treat it like a task when it's actually a tool. We cede control of our workday—and our to-do lists—to the dictates of others in pursuit of a mirage called "inbox zero." Rather than focusing mindfully on what's outgoing, we strive futilely to keep up with what's incoming.

Have our ambitions shrunk so small that this is actually a worthy goal? A goal for which we will thrust aside meaningful work along with the chance to do something good in this world? That may sound melodramatic, but can you deny that email distracts you from your creative ambitions on a daily basis?

In this book we'll flip the script on the way you approach email—shifting from a perspective of blind, numbers-based "productivity" to a mindset guided by your creative priorities. This is not simply a collection of rules for better email etiquette or whittling down the number of messages in your inbox; it is a guide to holistically revamping and repairing your relationship with email.

We will start at the root of the problem, taking a quick but eye-opening tour through the neuroscience and cultural baggage that shape our conflicted feelings about email. Next, we will build on that understanding to develop a new strategy for approaching our inboxes, one that focuses on putting the task of achieving meaningful work goals first and using email as a tool to achieve them.

Finally, we will proceed to a series of tips on style that will show you how to compose emails that will get the results you want, whether it's pitching an entrepreneur on investing in your startup or declining unwanted inquiries without guilt. And should you want to dig even deeper into the mechanics of email, a special, back-of-book "cheat sheets" section provides tactical scripts for sticky situations, everything from getting clients to pay you to managing angry customers.

By the time you finish *Unsubscribe* you will have mastered how to think about, manage, and write email with less anxiety and more grace, freeing you up to focus on the work that really matters—the stuff of building a legacy, not just keeping busy.

Contents

PART THREE: STYLE

PART FOUR: SUPERPOWERS

EXTRA CREDIT: CHEAT SHEETS

PART ONE: PSYCHOLOGY

WHY EMAIL MAKES US CRAZY

She checked her email too often, like a child eagerly tearing open a present she is not sure she wants.

—*Chimamanda Ngozie Adichie*[1]

Questioning Our Email Habits

To quote the great psychologist Ernest Becker, we are *choking on truth*.[2] In this Internet age we have so many answers, so much data at our fingertips, that it can be hard to remember the value of asking the right questions, of truly reflecting on a problem before you rush to fix it.

When it comes to our conflicted relationship with email, there are a number of nagging questions that merit deeper meditation: Why do minor misunderstandings in email inspire such outsize anxiety? Why do we feel like we owe everyone who emails us a response—and guilty if we can't give one? And why do we get such satisfaction from attaining "inbox zero," even when we know it's ultimately meaningless?

I believe that understanding *why* we behave in certain ways can be an incredibly powerful tool. Once you grasp the underlying motivations driving your actions, you are empowered to question those behaviors and react differently in the future. As Clayton Christensen, an eminent researcher on innovation, has said,

Questions are places in your mind where answers fit. If you haven't asked the question, the answer has nowhere to go. It hits your mind and bounces right off. You have to ask the question—you have to want to know—in order to open up the space for the answer to fit.[3]

So before we plunge into answers and how-to advice, let's examine exactly why email makes us so crazy. In the next few pages we'll dig into the strange brew of brain chemistry, social customs, and technology bias that drives our email obsession. Each essay will close with a question that's designed to crack open the way you think about email and offer a new perspective.

After you complete this little therapy session, you will have the proper foundation to begin building an effective email strategy and style as well as a wealth of ammunition for defending yourself against email's many psychological evils.

The Rat Brain: Why Email Is So Addictive

Everyone hates email. And yet we can't stop checking it. Recent studies show that office workers dip into their inboxes on average a whopping 74 times a day and spend roughly 28 percent of their total workday on the task of reading and responding to email. What's more, scientists have established a clear link between spending time on email and stress: the more frequently we check our email, the more frazzled we feel.[4]

It seems irrational. Why do we spend so much time doing something that has such a negative impact on our well-being? The fact of the matter is that even though we may not care for the content of every email we receive, many of us are addicted to the act of checking email. It activates a primal impulse in our brains to seek out rewards. And in this regard we're not very different from rats.

Back in the 1930s, psychologist B. F. Skinner invented a device called the "operant conditioning chamber," now known as the Skinner Box, which he used to test behavioral theories on rats. Skinner wanted to see what effect different kinds of positive reinforcements like food pellets and negative reinforcements like electric shocks would have on the animals.

First, he experimented with putting the rats on a *fixed schedule* of behavior reinforcement. For instance, if the rat pressed the lever inside the box, it would receive a food pellet. If it continued pressing the lever, every hundredth time the rat would receive another pellet. Press the lever 100 times, get a reward—that was the system.

Skinner also experimented with a *variable schedule*. In this scenario the rat didn't know when the reward was coming. It might have to press the lever 20 times to get a pellet, or it might have to press the lever 200 times to get a pellet. The system was random, and the rat could never know exactly when the reward was coming.

Surprisingly, the rats were significantly more motivated when they were on the variable schedule. Skinner found that even if he took away the rewards for the rats on the variable schedule, they would keep working, furiously pressing the lever for a very long time before giving up—much longer, in fact, than the rats on the fixed schedule would.

Is this starting to sound familiar yet? For better or worse, humans respond to positive rewards very similarly

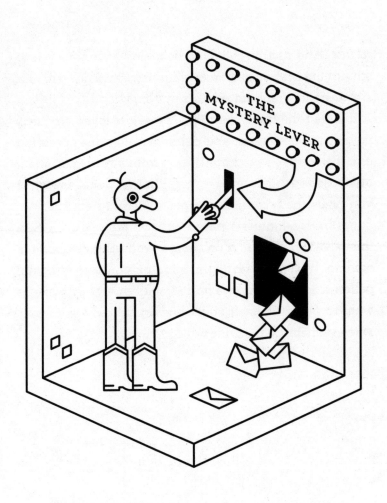

Do you want random rewards or real rewards?

to rats. And as Dan Ariely, a behavioral economist who studies the irrational actions of humans, explains: email is a near-perfect random rewards system.[5]

Most of the time when you "press the lever" to check your email messages, you get something disappointing or bothersome—a communication from a frustrated client or a boss with an urgent request. But every once in awhile you press the lever and you get something exciting—an email from a long-lost friend or, if you're really lucky, a video of goats jumping on things. And it's those random rewards, mixed in with all the mind-numbing updates and irksome requests, that we find so addictive. They make us want to push the lever again and again and again, even when we have better things to do.

Perspective Shift

Can you make a habit of identifying your "real rewards" at work in order to avoid falling into the trap of random rewards?

The rat brain is most likely to take control when you're feeling aimless. Steel yourself against idle email checking by making a ritual of jotting down tomorrow's to-do list before you leave the office each night. Creating your to-do list in advance empowers you to kick off the workday with clarity and momentum. It also means you have a framework in place for the day's priorities *before* you check your email, allowing you to weigh any incoming requests against what you've already planned to accomplish. As you craft your to-do list, remember to be realistic. Crossing everything off is your reward—and it will also reinforce the positive behavior.

The Progress Paradox:
Why Inbox Zero Is Irresistible

Alas, random rewards are not the whole story. There are still more unconscious forces at work, stoking our desire to relentlessly check email—namely, an innate urge to finish an activity once we've started it. When you recognize a task as complete, your brain releases the neurotransmitter dopamine, which makes you feel good and makes you want to repeat the behavior again to feel more pleasure.

Technologists long ago learned how to hack the brain's *urge to completion,* inventing a handy device now known as the progress bar.[6] They keep us glued to our computer screens as we track the status of our downloads; convince us to complete online surveys by making them seem as easy as one, two, three; and sucker us into filling out just a few more fields on our LinkedIn profiles to make them 100 percent complete.

Email taps into this urge to completion concept as well. Chipping away at our inbox gives us a sense of satisfaction precisely because the act includes such clear progress indicators. You started out with 232 email messages and now you have 50—progress! You're advancing toward

Inbox zero is an addictive game, not a meaningful goal.

that holy grail of email productivity, inbox zero, and your brain is compelling you to see the job through.

The problem is that while winnowing down your inbox gives you a strong feeling of progress, it's just that—a feeling. Because unread message counts do not obey the golden rule of progress bars: *Thou shalt not move backward.* Instead, your unread message count is always a moving target. While you attend to it, you have the false sensation of advancing toward a goal, but the moment you look away, the target shifts further into the distance as more messages roll in.

Conversely, when it comes to completing our most important creative projects, progress often feels elusive. The first reason is that completing meaningful work takes time—often weeks, months, or even years. While you can complete a social media profile or tackle a handful of unread emails in a matter of minutes, finishing big projects frequently takes so long that we lose sight of how far we've come. There's no built-in progress bar when you're on the long journey of writing a book, coding an iPhone app, or brainstorming the right business model to raise funding.

The second reason is that the applications we use to do our most meaningful work often "hide" progress from us.

When we write a shitty first draft in Word or Google Docs, we highlight it, erase it, and begin again in the same file until we get it right. By the time you get to the finished product it's as if the first, second, third, and fourth efforts never happened. Those versions have simply vanished. Similarly, we cut and paste away our progress in numerous other apps, from Photoshop to PowerPoint, on an hourly basis. And even if you are meticulous enough to maintain separate versions of your files, they're usually tucked away in a digital folder that's out of sight, out of mind.

This is the progress paradox: by dint of technology, it's easy to see our progress when we're doing relatively meaningless short-term tasks, while it's quite difficult to see our progress when we're engaged in the long-term, creative projects that will ultimately have the most impact on our lives.

Perspective Shift

How can you create a tangible sense of progress within the context of the projects that matter most to you?

Staying engaged with meaningful work—and fending off the allure of email—is all about making progress visible. A few tips and tricks you can explore: post a calendar by your desk to track your daily creative output, such as the number of words you wrote, bugs you fixed, or sales calls you made; break large projects down into weekly milestones that you can tick off so you have a continuous sense of achievement; take five minutes at the end of your day to journal about your "small wins"[7] and acknowledge the steps you made toward your goal; or print out your drafts, sketches, and prototypes as they accrue and keep them in an ever-growing stack on your desk as a testament to your progress. The key is to invent "progress hacks" to make your meaningful work as addictive as email.

The Negativity Bias: Why Our Words Betray Us

When it comes to delicate interactions, email seems to act like some strange form of kryptonite. How many times have you received a poorly worded message that sent you into a fit of anger? What about sending an email that you didn't think twice about only to have the receiver respond with a level of outrage that seemed completely out of proportion? What is it about email that makes us so socially inept?

At the core of the problem is a lack of social feedback. Normally when we communicate with someone in person or even on the phone, we are reading a thousand little social cues as we talk and deciding what to do next based on those cues. It often happens that we will start to say something but then, based on nonverbal feedback we get from the other person, think better of it and take another tack.

When we communicate through email, however, that social feedback loop is absent. Rather than proceeding by baby steps—I speak, you react, and then I adapt my response or clarify—I, the sender, just blurt everything out at you, the receiver, and hope for the best. What's more, as we compose our emails, we do so assuming the other person is still getting all of the peripheral social cues from us that they would receive in a normal face-to-face interaction.

Daniel Goleman, the psychologist who brought the phrase "emotional intelligence" into common parlance, looked into this phenomenon and discovered something fascinating: people have what he calls a natural *negativity bias* toward email.[8] Goleman found that if the sender felt positive about an email, then the receiver usually just felt neutral. And if the sender felt neutral about the message, then the receiver typically felt negative about it. In other words, email really *is* like kryptonite when it comes to expressing positive emotions: it's as if every message you send gets automatically downgraded a few positivity notches by the time someone else receives it.

We've all experienced this: you draft an email, think it's perfectly fine, and send it off only to later have the receiver take offense at a message you thought was innocuous. What Goleman's research reveals is that the recipient is not actually being oversensitive, or at least not any more sensitive than the next guy. The fact of the matter is that everyone is extra-sensitive about tone in emails because they don't provide the key ingredient in successful

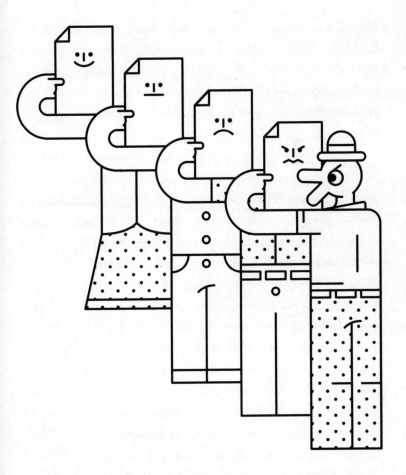

Amp up your emotional intelligence when emailing
or suffer the consequences.

social interactions: real-time feedback. Emails lack the facial expressions, physical gestures, and vocal tone that typically shape our interpretation of what someone is saying and allow us to adjust our delivery in order to get the true meaning across. And in absence of those cues, we tend to assume the worst.

Which brings us to one of the most contentious issues in all of email: to use or not to use emoticons and exclamation points. Those who argue strongly against using one or the other often believe that doing so is unprofessional. But does this claim actually hold water?

In the context of a message that is likely to be received negatively—read: all email messages—the judicious use of emoticons and exclamation points can act as a useful counter-balance for tone. In essence, they function as a sort of shorthand for social cues, conveying that you are playful, excited, enthusiastic, or supportive without requiring you to be overly wordy. And by more accurately conveying your real intentions, you increase the chances that your email will be well received, making it more likely to get the response you want. Is that unprofessional?

Of course, I understand the impulse to reject these cheery tools. Certainly there was a time when I thought using either of the two Es was beneath me. But after 15-plus years of managing clients, writers, designers, and speakers remotely via email, I can happily say I've been disabused of that notion. I've had to cajole, convince, and critique hundreds of people who worked for me or way above me, and I couldn't have done it successfully without embedding a lot of supportive social cues into my email messages.

The negativity bias is real, and any tools that can help us overcome it should be considered fair game.* Getting shit done is much more professional than sticking to silly principles that don't make sense.

------

*There are of course a few caveats for the use of emoticons and exclamation points: the two Es should always be used sparingly. Emoticons do not mean emojis, which are not professional for anyone outside your innermost circle of colleagues. And you should always wait to break out the emoticons until you know the person you're communicating with. Just as you wouldn't wink at someone during a job interview, neither should you wink at them in your outreach email.

Perspective Shift

What if we took care to communicate not just information but also empathy in our emails?

When we take the negativity bias into account, it's clear that emailing effectively requires us to upgrade the positivity of our language. Better outcomes will arise from being more explicit about the emotional intent of our messages and more considerate of our recipient's feelings. Although it might not seem intuitive at first, taking the time to show empathy and encouragement in your emails can actually make you more efficient. Your clients and colleagues are much more likely to respond to your requests if they feel like you're on their side.

The Rule of Reciprocity:
Why Inbox Overload Gives Us a Guilt Complex

Like it or not, email breeds a curiously strong sense of obligation. The more unread messages we have in our inboxes, the more guilty we feel. The more time that passes before we can reply to a message, the more we apologize. How many times have you started an email with, *I'm sorry I couldn't get back to you sooner but* ... ? Somewhere deep down we truly feel that we owe everyone a response.

For family, friends, and coworkers this seems natural. We have long-standing relationships with them, so feeling an obligation to reply to their messages makes sense. But what about complete strangers? Why do we feel guilty if we can't respond to someone we don't even know?

Numerous experiments have shown that humans tend to adhere to the *rule of reciprocity* in social interactions. At its most basic level this means that we want to respond to a positive action with another positive action. If someone does a favor for us, we want to return the favor, even if—and this is the crucial distinction—that favor wasn't something we necessarily wanted.[9]

Sociologist Phillip Kunz proved the unexpected power

of the rule of reciprocity with an unusual, DIY experiment back in the 1970s.[10] He made up hundreds of holiday greetings, with each including either a handwritten note or a card and a picture of Kunz and his family. Then, around Christmastime he mailed the holiday cards to 600 perfect strangers.

Amazingly, a wave of replies started coming in soon afterward. Some people responded with lengthy three- to four-page letters updating him on their lives, while others sent pictures and shared news of their families. Kunz ended up receiving over 200 responses in total. Even more incredibly, he continued to receive holiday cards from many of those "strangers" for another 15 years.

Would you respond to a holiday card from a stranger? The mere notion probably sounds laughable in these days of dwindling snail mail. But what about replying to an email from a stranger? I bet you've already done it many times and will no doubt do so again in the near future.

Although we might not think of getting an email from a stranger as a "favor," the rule of reciprocity isn't always rational. The mere fact that someone took the time to write to you activates a deep-seated social behavior, the desire to reciprocate like with like. In most social situations, of course, this is good—it leads to the type of cooperative human behavior that has served us well as a species.

Yet in the context of email it can bite us in the ass. Not because email shouldn't adhere to the same conventions as other social interactions but because email isn't subject to the same physical constraints as other social interactions. For instance, you used to have to meet someone in person to get their mailing address—or at least find a printed directory for their city—which would then enable you to send them a holiday card. (Kunz, for instance, found his test subjects in the phone book.) But no one needs to meet you in person to get your email address; if it's posted on your website, anyone who has access to the Internet has access to you. And the barrier to entry is lower too: you don't have to worry about finding stationery or having good handwriting or paying postage. All of which leads to an imbalance in how much email you can receive (a seemingly infinite amount) and how much you can actually respond to (a limited amount).

This is where advances in technology clash with the rule of reciprocity. We still feel a strong desire to reciprocate when someone sends us a message, yet we rarely have the bandwidth to respond to every single message. Ergo: guilt.

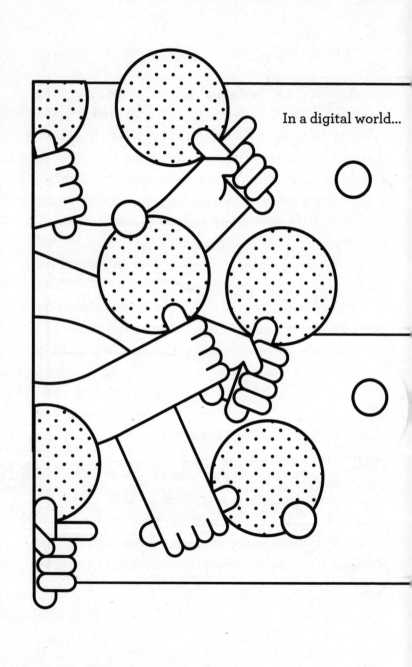

In a digital world...

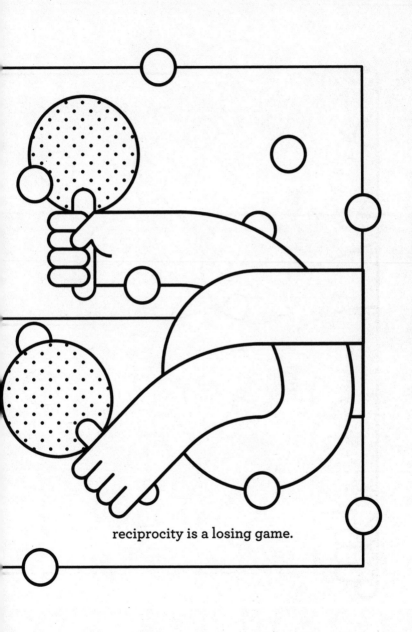

reciprocity is a losing game.

Perspective Shift

What if you pictured the messages in your inbox like a stack of real, physical mail?

If you got 200+ letters a day, you would never think it was realistic to respond to all of them. Why should email be any different? Your time is limited, and you can only respond to so much. Visualizing your email as a physical object gives you a more realistic understanding of how possible—or impossible—reciprocity really is. This encourages you to make hard choices about which messages deserve a hand-crafted response, which can tolerate a templated reply, and which do not warrant a response at all. Politely responding to every single email you receive is all well and good, but not if it makes you a stranger to your own goals.

The Asker's Advantage:
Why We Can't Just Say No

Email is an excellent medium for asking but an awful one for declining. See if this scenario rings a bell: Someone sends you a message asking you to do something. You feel annoyed that they would ask you to do such a thing, because you don't have the time, the money, or the energy—and *don't they know that?!* And yet you agree to do the thing. Then, later, when said obligation rolls around, you kick yourself for having agreed to it.

No doubt most of us have succumbed to this little cycle of email martyrdom more than a few times. But what makes it so appealing? Why do we have so much trouble saying no, especially in instances when we thought the request was a bit presumptuous in the first place?

In a now-classic MetaFilter post, Andrea Donderi theorizes that everyone is raised as either an *asker* or a *guesser*.[11] In an ask culture you are taught that asking for whatever you need is fine, with the understanding that the person you're asking can always decline. In a guess culture you are taught that you should only ask for something if you think you are very likely to get a yes. In other words, you are trained to be attentive to subtle details and signs that will help you assess the likelihood that someone will be receptive to your proposal.

The problem emerges when askers confront guessers. Askers are inclined to just "put it out there" no matter what and leave the decision up to you: *Can I crash in your studio apartment for a week? Will you code my website for free? Could you donate money to my new business venture?* You get the idea.

Askers don't mind if you say no because they were just testing the waters. But guessers have trouble believing that. They naturally assume that askers share their mindset, so they don't think someone would ask for something if they didn't expect to get a yes. Thus, when askers collide with guessers, their requests can often come off as brazen or presumptuous.

It goes without saying that this dynamic unfolds on email on a daily basis. A guesser gets a request from an asker, and it sends them into a huff: *How could they think I would just agree to? . . . Do they think I have extra time to burn? How could they assume? . . .* And so forth. Before you know it—and I speak as a patent guesser here—you're cycling through an unproductive spiral of possible responses

Are you letting a bunch of "askers" push you around?

to an email you didn't expect and ignoring the things you should actually be doing.

But if you take a step back and remember the askers vs guessers distinction, it's much easier to shrug off requests you previously would have found exceedingly annoying. It also frees you up to decline those requests without feeling put upon.

Once you start thinking of the irksome email requests you get as someone just throwing spaghetti at the wall and thinking, *Who knows what they'll say? I'll just give it a shot!*, it really takes the pressure off. You no longer assume they're expecting you to say yes, and it becomes much easier to say no.

A nice benefit of adding the askers vs guessers concept to your arsenal is that it also frees you up to feel more carefree about asking on your own behalf. Being able to adopt the mindset of an asker who thinks—*What's the worst that could happen? They say no. So what?*—is a practical attitude for everything from using email to get what you want, to getting a date, to negotiating a better salary. Because, let's face it: in a can-do culture like America's, the world is the asker's oyster.

Perspective Shift

What if you stepped into the asker's shoes every time you got an email that felt like an imposition?

Rather than assuming the sender expects you to say yes—and resenting the unwanted obligation—assume he thinks it's a long shot. Reframing the situation like this makes it easier to put the ask in perspective and consider the opportunity with a relaxed attitude. Once you level the playing field between the possibility of saying yes and the possibility of saying no, it becomes easier to gracefully decline inquiries that don't align with your priorities. Remember, email martyrdom doesn't increase your productivity; it only increases your blood pressure. Acknowledge that you always have a choice in what you take on—and make it.

PART TWO: STRATEGY

HOW TO EMAIL SMARTER, FASTER, AND LESS

It helps to ask, "What's the worst thing that happens if I don't answer this email?"

—*Tavi Gevinson*[12]

The Physics of Email

Newton's Third Law of Motion says that *for every action, there is an equal and opposite reaction.* The physics of email is no different: the more email you send, the more email you will receive. The better you give, the better you get.

We know this intuitively, and yet in the face of a never-ending onslaught of messages, we often ignore this simple principle. We feel an obligation to respond to every email we receive—*and quickly*—often to the detriment of our own workflow and priorities, not to mention the quality of the response itself.

The first step to mastering email is to understand that you are in the driver's seat. You—and no one else—choose what to respond to and when. You don't have to *do* anything.

What's more, the style, frequency, and rhythm of your messages directly impact what comes back to you. Each time you send an email, you are also sending something else: a subtle signal that sets expectations with your colleagues, clients, and customers.

Did you respond right away? Five hours later? A week later? Did you dash off a quick, pass-the-buck email that fails to clarify anything? Or did you wait to reply until you could send a thoughtful and complete message?

Every action you take sets others' expectations for the future. If every time you get a message from a client, you respond within 15 minutes, that client will begin to *expect* you to respond within 15 minutes —and potentially be upset when you don't. That's why proactively setting expectations for yourself and those around you about how and when you will use email in advance of sitting down at your desk every day is essential.

That said, you can't very well set expectations for anyone if you don't know what you're doing in the grand scheme of things. Thus, we'll start this section on strategy by zooming out to take in the big picture: determining what goals and relationships are important to you. Then we'll zoom in to get tactical by crafting a daily routine that will help you balance meaningful work with your email obligations, prioritize and respond to messages efficiently, and dispatch unwanted emails without guilt.

WTF Are You Trying to Accomplish Anyway?

You may hate spending all of your time on email, but it's very hard to stop doing so unless you have a clear idea of *what you would rather be doing*. Nor can you decide which emails are important and which are not if you do not know what you're trying to accomplish.

That's why we're going to pause for a moment and direct our attention away from email to that mysterious quantity I keep referring to as "meaningful work." This is the type of work that contributes to your legacy, helps you advance your career, or expands your skill set. When you finish such work, you have the satisfying feeling of time well spent and a job well done.

Email can certainly assist you in doing such work, but it rarely qualifies as meaningful work in and of itself. Let's talk about what does qualify so we can develop a clearer sense of where you would prefer to focus your energies. There are three categories into which meaningful work usually falls:

Mission-based work. In standard career-advice speak, this is what's described as "finding your calling." Inventor

Elon Musk wants to *create a true spacefaring civilization*, activist Malala Yousafzai wants to *educate and empower the millions of girls who are currently denied schooling*, and chef Jamie Oliver wants to *increase the health and well-being of future generations by providing better food education*. These sorts of goals are impressive, if not intimidating. But if you don't have some change-the-world-level life mission, don't sweat it—not everyone needs a calling.

Project-based work. This category of work aspiration is simply to complete a given project. A project can be anything: maybe you want to *get a job at Facebook, raise $100,000 in funding for your startup, land a big client*, or *write a book*. Most of the meaningful work we do relates to completing some sort of long-term project, whether it's something smaller like *writing a thoughtful blog post* or a bit bigger like *launching a website*. Projects can be any level of ambition, but they typically require a number of steps to complete. You don't have to change the world; you just have to finish them.

Skills-based work. The last category is work that enhances your skill set. Perhaps you want to *learn how to extend your design skills to mobile, master a new coding language, get better at negotiating,* or *improve your writing ability*. Again, any level of ambition is fine here; the point is you're doing tasks that help you grow professionally and/or personally.

When you're determining what meaningful work looks like for you, it will typically be some combination of items in the above categories. So for instance, I might say that on a mission level *I want to help people find more meaning and creativity in their work lives.* On a project level I am working on two things right now: *finishing this book* and *building a new website*. On a skills level I would like to *get better at promoting my work* and to *hone my public speaking ability*.

When you contemplate your own goals you will probably arrive at a similar sort of list. Some people have the luxury of focusing on just one thing (e.g., Musk's grand spacefaring mission!), but most of us are juggling a

Which emails align with your meaningful work goals?

variety of goals and ambitions at any given moment. The important thing is to keep your list relatively short. You'll note I have two projects I'm working on, both of which directly relate to my mission, and two skills I'd like to improve, both of which are related to my projects: building a new website challenges me to get better at promoting my work, and finishing this book could lead to more speaking opportunities.

Clarifying what meaningful work means to you by setting specific, measurable goals lends a powerful sense of purpose to your workday. On one hand, it provides a countervailing force to the addictive pull of email by giving you somewhere more rewarding to focus your energy. On the other, it helps you swiftly prioritize your messages when you do turn your attention to your inbox by providing a yardstick for assessing the relevance of those emails to the work that matters most to you.

If you want to say no to email, you must say yes to something else. What projects do you want to move forward? What are you trying to accomplish?

ACTIVITY

After the requisite soul searching, write down your meaningful work goals for the next three months.

Any mix of mission, project, and skill goals is fine. Be realistic about what you can achieve, and keep the list short—no more than three to four goals total. Post the list somewhere visible from your desk, and refer to it regularly as you make your daily to-do lists and process your email. If your meaningful goals are always top of mind, it becomes much easier to spend your time more wisely.

Who Are the People That Matter?

All email messages are not created equal. A message from your boss is not the same as a message from a persnickety former client is not the same as a message from someone you've never met. Your relationship to the person emailing you should govern its importance—or lack thereof.

Now that you've put some thought into *what* you want to accomplish at work, the next step is to focus on *who* is important to your work. In order to be able to process your email efficiently you need to create a mental hierarchy of the people who email you and determine their relative importance.

This is the simple framework I use for breaking my email contacts down into a few distinct buckets:

VIPs. At the top of the chain you have VIPs. These are the people closest to you whose messages need immediate attention. They are the people you depend upon for love and your livelihood; no one is more important. VIPs typically include folks like your boss, big-deal clients, and your spouse or significant other. They are the people who you want to feel taken care of at all costs. You will generally want to respond to them the same day and ideally within a few hours. This list should be short and sweet, perhaps three to five people. If you conclude that everybody is really important, you haven't decided anything.

Key collaborators. At the next level you have key collaborators. These are people with whom you work closely who require timely responses for projects and relationships to move forward. Key collaborators normally include colleagues you work with regularly, smaller clients with active projects, and close advisers, friends, or family. Depending on the pace of your work, this group usually needs a response within one to three days. This list can be slightly larger than your VIPs, and the size will vary based on the scope of your work (e.g., you might have two close colleagues or twenty-five, depending on your situation). Still, endeavor to keep it lean.

Fun people. Beneath essential collaborators you have the best category in the email hierarchy: fun people. These are the folks with whom communicating is more enjoyable than necessary. They are the loose set of friends, acquaintances, and colleagues who bring laughter and insight into your inbox. You don't communicate with them because it's imperative but because it's enjoyable and sustaining. For this group responding quickly is a low priority and depends on your availability. If you're busy, waiting a week or two to get back to them is fine. This list can be any length but with the understanding that you would do well to choose wisely. Even if it's infrequently, you are choosing to give these people your valuable time and energy.

Potentials. After fun people you have potentials. This group is composed of all of the people who *could* be important or useful in the future, but you're not sure yet. It includes prospective clients, potential employers and allies, and new contacts of all kinds who arrive in your inbox with an endorsement from a trustworthy source, perhaps via an introduction from a close friend or business associate. You'll typically want to respond to potentials within a few days or less, as it's good to keep the momentum going in the early stages of an email exchange with someone you've never met. Note that the potentials list is less a fixed category than one that people flow through before landing in one of the other four groups: VIP, key, fun, or random. After a few messages you should be able to assess the potential of the new relationship properly and file the individual in the relevant fixed category.

Randoms. On the lowest level you have randoms. These are all of the people, good and bad, who enter your inbox uninvited and unverified by a trusted contact. They are generally asking you to do things outside of the scope of your current work. It could be someone inviting you to do an exciting speaking gig, a distant colleague working on an unrelated project asking you to brainstorm, or a young person who respects your know-how asking for advice. You have little to no control over how many random people crowd into your inbox. What you do have control over is how you choose to respond—and if you respond at all. The people in this group have no priority until you assign it. You might choose to respond to an unexpected but valuable opportunity the next day while shelving an unsolicited request for response in two weeks if you have the time. Be wary of letting random emails chip away at your productivity—life is too short to let strangers dictate what you do with your day.

ACTIVITY

Think about the people who regularly email you and then segment them into the three core groups: VIPs, key collaborators, and fun people (skip randoms for now).

The challenge here is to keep each list as short as possible by making hard choices about who really matters. When you're at your busiest, having this hierarchy in mind will help you quickly prioritize which emails are truly urgent or important and which are just noise.

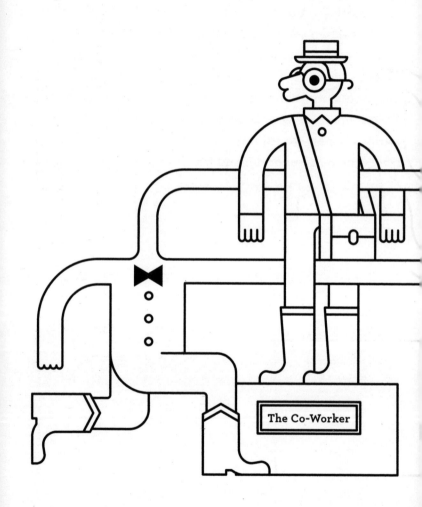

The Co-Worker

Crafting a Daily Email Routine

Email can take up as much or as little of your day as you choose. How much time you spend on it is really a question of self-control, which is why it's crucial to devise a daily routine for checking email and to understand the obstacles that can throw you off course.

Once you have a system in place that works with your natural creative rhythms and sets expectations for those you work with, it becomes exponentially easier to stay focused and execute the tasks that really matter. Here's how to get started.

Start your day with meaningful work. Despite the fact that one in two people look at their email before breakfast, it is rarely productive to check your email first thing in the morning.[13] In fact, it's usually counter-productive to start your day by letting other people's demands set your priorities. Instead, devote the first 60–90 minutes of your day to a task that advances your meaningful work goals. This way you are doing your most important and challenging work when your brainpower is at its peak rather than later in the day, when you're harried and your energy is depleted. It also means that when you do turn your attention to email, no matter what you find there—what fires you have to put out, what unwanted questions you have to respond to—you've already gotten some good work done that day.

Side note: If you must conduct your meaningful work in the afternoon due to immovable morning obligations, try doing a "reboot ritual" to clear your mind before you begin. Ten minutes of meditation, a brisk walk around the block, or a power nap are all good options.

Don't check your email more than two to three times a day. There are two types of emailers: reactors, who rely on notifications and near-constant monitoring of their inboxes to nibble away at their email throughout the day, and batchers, who set aside specific chunks of time to power through their email so they can ignore it the rest of the day. Not surprisingly, batchers are significantly more effective when it comes to getting shit done, and according to recent research, they're also less stressed.[14] To get yourself into the groove of batching, I recommend setting aside 30–60 minutes in the late morning and a similar amount of time in the mid- to late afternoon for checking email. Depending on the volume of email you receive, you might want to add a third and final email processing window at the close of your workday to tie up loose ends and leave work with a clear conscience.

Specify blocks of time for batch processing your email and put them on your calendar. By setting aside time on your calendar you explicitly commit to devoting a certain amount of energy to email. Because you have time set aside to process your inbox, it's easier to move forward with other tasks, knowing that you'll have time to tend to your email later. More importantly, it also requires you to commit to blocks of time when you are *not* checking email.

Extra credit: I would also recommend carving out blocks of time on your calendar for meaningful work, even if it's just once a day first thing in the morning. If we don't explicitly plan to do the work that matters, it tends to fall by the wayside. Putting something on your calendar means you are committing to it.

Treat your calendar time blocks like actual meetings. That means you show up, you start on time, and you

Creating limitations for email can be liberating.

finish on time. There may not be other people present at this "meeting," but the point is to respect your time just as you would respect someone else's at a meeting. If you've scheduled a block of time for meaningful work, give it all of your attention and effort. Don't give up if it takes 10–20 minutes to get in the zone, and don't be afraid to lock yourself in a conference room if necessary. Exercise the same discipline with your email blocks: when your scheduled time is up, stop checking your email and move on. This forces you to prioritize who you respond to and at what length—a useful skill.

Use VIP email notifications. If you'd like to stick to specific blocks of time for checking email but you have a special someone who will freak out if you don't tend to their email within five minutes of receiving it, compromise by using VIP notifications. On an iPhone you can designate certain people as VIPs so their emails go to a separate VIP inbox. You can also configure your notifications to play a special tone when that inbox gets a message. If you have an Android phone, you can use the Gmail app to set up a similar system for notifications when messages arrive from predesignated priority senders. This method helps you ignore your email when you need to without worrying you'll miss something crucial.

Avoid leaving your email open in the background. Research has shown that just having your email program open in the background of your computer screen as you focus on another task, even if the window is minimized, can decrease performance.[15] Even if your email isn't front and center, your brain still knows it's there in the background and devotes a certain amount of energy to monitoring it, which takes away from your ability to truly execute the task at hand. Avoid such distractions by quarantining your email in a separate area from your main workspace. This might mean setting up a separate monitor just for email or checking your email only on a mobile phone or tablet. Checking your email in a physically separate space can actually make your incoming messages—and any attendant anxiety or urgency—feel more distant and less pressing. The more clear your primary work screen is, the more serene your mind is.[16]

Mind the switching costs. Every time you stop doing a task you are working on to check your email, you incur what researchers call a "switching cost." Particularly if you're doing any kind of work that requires deep concentration (aka creative flow) such as writing, coding, or assembling a presentation, it typically takes at least 25 minutes to get properly back into the task after you've interrupted yourself.[17] Even worse, multiple studies have shown that the more frequently you check your email, the less productive you are *and* the less happy you are.[18] That's a huge price to pay for a quick glance at your inbox.

Be aware that willpower declines over the course of the day. We do not have an infinite supply of willpower. Every time you exert your willpower during your workday, you have a little bit less left over. When it comes to email this means it becomes more difficult to resist the temptation to check it as the day goes on. It also becomes more challenging to make good decisions and compose messages as your best self. As willpower wanes, our email weaknesses loom large, and we risk giving in to our penchant for gossipy remarks, cutting sarcasm, dictatorial language, or a good old-fashioned flame war. The good news is that once you're aware of the rhythms of willpower, you can use them to your advantage: try using your late-morning email block to respond to the messages that demand a maximum of craft and composure and your afternoon block to reply to relatively mindless emails.

Set expectations publicly. Once you've defined your email schedule, tell people about it. I cannot stress how helpful it is to openly discuss communication ground rules with bosses, coworkers, and clients *before* problems arise. Ask your boss how swiftly you need to respond to her emails—within 15 minutes? 60 minutes? 24 hours? outside of work? You may be surprised by her answer or you may be disappointed, but at least you'll know. Share your work practices with coworkers so they understand how to best communicate with you and you with them, such as asking them to *email you with nonurgent questions and come to your desk with urgent ones.* Tell your clients upfront what kind of response time they can expect from you—for example, a *same-day response on emails before 3 p.m. while their project is active*—before they come to a different conclusion on their own. If you don't want to be available on email at all hours, you need to proactively set expectations with others and stick to them religiously.

Activity

Map two weeks of work onto your calendar. Include time blocks for checking email, doing meaningful work, and any other activities, like meetings or client calls, that are an essential part of your workday.

Make sure you don't schedule everything back-to-back; instead, deliberately build in some slack time each day so you have windows to rest and recover, deal with unexpected interruptions, or react to urgent situations on the fly without sabotaging your routine. You'll also want to account for the fact that willpower and focus typically wane as the day goes on. Scheduling demanding tasks for earlier in the day and easier tasks for later on is ideal. Try to adhere to this schedule for the full two weeks, and see if you aren't significantly more productive in the work that really matters to you.

Processing Your Inbox with Poise

Not everything is urgent. This is the mantra you must internalize to take control of your email. Of course, the challenge is that most everyone who sends you a message tends to be convinced that their correspondence truly *is* urgent. Managing this balancing act between your actual workload and your inbox overload is the essence of prioritization.

As you decide who to respond to and when, keep in mind that these hungry email masses who think their messages are so urgent have no idea what your real workload is. They don't know you have 224 other emails to respond to, that you are on a huge deadline for a challenging project, that your boss is breathing down your neck about that proposal, and that you already have a full to-do list for the day.

So you have to prioritize their emails against *what you know you have to do* rather than *what they want you to do*. Otherwise you'll spend the bulk of your day fielding other people's requests and never finding the time to accomplish something you can call your own.

At the same time, considering the other person's perspective and responding with politeness and respect need never fall by the wayside, not to mention that acting with these qualities in mind will make email more bearable for everyone. Here's a short checklist of bad habits to avoid and simple tricks to consider as you process your email during your scheduled time blocks.

Don't let default settings dictate your workflow. The easiest way to fail at email is to accept your inbox "as is." Every app, from Outlook to Gmail, has default settings that are tailor-made to sabotage your focus. We often accept these features as immutable, feeling helpless to change them. Yet even the tiniest tweaks can result in an exponential increase in productivity. Here's one common scenario: Let's say you use Outlook, which means your work email and your calendar live in a single app. You don't want to leave your email open all the time, but if you close Outlook, you won't get meeting reminders! In order to have your calendar open, you suffer through a distracting stream of constant email notifications on a daily basis. This can be easily solved by *not* defaulting to using

Outlook for your calendar; instead, download a separate calendar app and configure it to work with your email. Then you can keep your calendar app open—and get the proper meeting notifications—without being beholden to your email at all times.

Another common "default" affliction is using a single inbox folder to manage all email activity. Not surprisingly, a recent study reported that workers feel "lost in email" about 23 percent of the time.[19] If that sounds like you, you might benefit from implementing a folder structure that helps you sift and sort your email in a more organized manner, setting up folders for messages that you need to reply to (Reply), are awaiting a response from someone else (Waiting), or you might reference later (Archive). In a world where you can Google a solution to almost any problem, there's no excuse for sitting on your hands: figure out what default settings aren't working for you and then fix them.

Extra Credit: For my personal recs on the best calendar apps to supplement your email and different folder structures that might inspire you, see the "Resources" section on page 211.

Decide if email is the appropriate medium for your response. As discussed earlier, email is an imperfect medium for communication because it lacks social cues, leading us to lean toward a negative interpretation of its content. Email, therefore, is *not* good for delicate conversations, criticizing someone's behavior, debating contentious issues, and so forth. This we know. But don't forget that email is also terrible for brainstorming ideas, discussing dependencies, or doing any kind of complex planning or decision-making. For all of these types of discussions a quick face-to-face meeting or phone call is wildly more efficient. Make a practice of regularly taking the initiative to move such conversations offline. You'll be rescuing yourself and everyone else from those annoying email threads that drag on for 15 to 20 messages and constantly interrupt you throughout the day.

Cross-reference against your list of "people who matter." Not everyone who emails you warrants the same response time—or perhaps any response at all. As you process your messages make sure you are also taking into account your relationship to the sender of the email. In

Be a warrior, not a worrier.

other words, don't prioritize responding to someone you've never met over responding to your boss, and don't prioritize responding to a random pitch over responding to your coworker who needs help on a project. Your working life and your credibility are built on relationships—be mindful of them.

Close conversations at the earliest opportunity. The best way to get less email is to send less email. A great way to do this is to proactively close the conversation as soon as it's convenient. This means always striving to respond to emails completely, cutting off the possibility of a long back-and-forth. For example, let's say a colleague emails you asking if you want to go to lunch next week, and you write back, *Sure!* You know, of course, that he will now have to write you back asking what time is good for you, and the email thread will get longer. Why not just advance the conversation from the get-go by writing: *Sure! What about next Thursday 9/1 at 12:30pm at the Corner Bistro?* Now you've preempted additional emails about the date, time, and location, allowing the recipient to just respond: *Sounds great. See you there.* And now you're done instead of having to email ten more times.

Dispatch easy emails first. Productivity guru David Allen has a two-minute rule that is useful for powering through your inbox quickly. The idea is if you can respond in two minutes, go ahead and do it right away because it will take more effort to come back to it, reprocess the email thread, and respond later. This does not mean you should respond to *all emails* that take less than two minutes; rather, it means that you should respond to all of the emails that you can process quickly and that relate to people who matter or your meaningful work goals. Less relevant and/or random emails should always be left for last and filed under *If I have time*.

Decrease urgency by sending quick expectation-setting replies. Sometimes you're well aware that your sender feels her message is urgent, but you just can't get to it right away because you have more important things to do. Even so, setting aside the message until later can be difficult because you feel the nagging psychic pull of someone anxiously awaiting a response. In this situation the best approach is to respond immediately with a short message that provides context and lets her know when you *will* be able to answer her message in full.

Let's say you receive an urgent request from a regular customer. You might reply:

Hi Elizabeth—I got this message, and I understand your concern. I'm stuck in a meeting until 4 p.m., but I'll address this and respond in more detail as soon as it wraps up. Thanks for your patience!

Or perhaps an old colleague wants to schedule a catch-up call but your plate is already full:

Hi Walter—Thanks for reaching out. I would love to catch up! However, I'm currently on deadline for a huge project, and I don't have any bandwidth for the next week. I'll reach back out when my schedule frees up, and we'll book a time. Looking forward to it.

People crave context. If you merely help them understand where their email sits within your workload, they can be surprisingly understanding. What's more, expectation-setting emails can help *you* relax by allowing you to reassert control over your schedule and release any feeling of obligation about meeting someone else's timetable.

Let go of inbox zero. Remember that your unread message count is not an audit of your productivity. (Zero, quite literally, means nothing.) Although it can be satisfying in the short term, attaining inbox zero is cold comfort in the long term. If you want to make time to accomplish meaningful work, you have to let go of the notion of an empty inbox. If you can accept that it's just not going to happen, you've taken the first step toward removing yourself from the productivity rat race. In the grand scheme of things email is just one small part of doing great work.

ACTIVITY

Conduct an email audit for one week, noting down any recurring anxieties, distractions, or inbox roadblocks as they surface.

Once you have a sense of what's tripping you up, address it head on. Perhaps you'll find that every time you open your email to respond to existing messages, you get sidetracked by new incoming messages. In this case you might start using Outlook's Work Offline feature when you check your email, or download the Inbox Pause browser extension for Gmail. Or you might notice you have trouble finding certain emails that you need to refer to again and again and decide to create a reference folder where you stash them for easy access. Constant optimization is the key to productivity. What can you tweak?

Finessing the Follow-Up

Emails are usually about asking. Either someone is asking you for something—to do a task, consider an offer, or share a piece of information—or you are asking them.

No ask is complete until it has an answer, and yet many of us treat email as if it were a one-and-done proposition. You shoot off an email with your request, and now the ball is in their court. It's on them to notice your email, thoughtfully consider it, and respond in a timely fashion, right?

Wrong. Assuming that anyone has the wherewithal—or even the obligation—to respond to your email is a recipe for failure. We're all busy and distracted and overwhelmed, and that means things slip through the cracks. It's no one's fault, but it is a fact. That means you need to have a system for tracking pending items.

Many of the things you ask for in emails are linked to a task you need to get done: you need to book a venue for a party so you email the venue asking for a quote, you need to upgrade your version of WordPress so you email your web developer asking her to do it, and so forth. But merely sending the email does not mean these tasks are done—what they are is pending completion. This means you need to keep monitoring them to ensure they *do* get done.

This kind of conscientious follow-up is a skill that is overlooked and underrated by many. But I can't stress enough how important it is to getting things done, both in the world of email and the great wide world beyond. A few pointers on following up effectively:

Don't be shy. Some people hesitate to follow up because they think it would be intrusive or off-putting. But typically the opposite is true: rather than viewing such persistence as annoying, most professionals view follow-up as a sign of passion and initiative. Speaking personally, I have hired people, responded to sales pitches, and taken time out to offer advice precisely because someone pursued me with an alacrity that caught my attention. Follow-up shows that you genuinely care. (That being said, too much follow-up won't endear you to anyone. One or two follow-up messages, appropriately spaced out, is typically a good threshold before you tip into the category of truly annoying.)

Consider your timing. As we are all well aware, there are certain times of the day and week when our influx of email is particularly intense as well as times when people are less likely to be focused on work. Everyone has a lot of email on Monday mornings, for instance, and most everyone is a bit checked out on Friday afternoons and weekends. If you're extremely keen to get a response, time your follow-up for a moment when the recipient is likely to be paying attention. In my experience this means sending your email outside of normal work hours, either very early in the morning or later in the evening.

Offer a concise recap. Some people follow up by merely forwarding their original email and saying, *Hey, did you get a chance to look at this?* Now, if that person didn't respond to your email the first time, resending the same message is probably not going to get better results the second time. Instead, forward your original email as a record, but write a new message on top that rephrases your ask in a more concise manner, ideally so that the recipient can skim the follow-up email and respond without reading down the thread. If the original message was long, just say something like, *See details below.*

Productivity requires persistence.

Add a new angle. Although you should never assume that your recipient actually read your first email, there's always a chance they did—and they didn't respond because it wasn't compelling. Without making your email too lengthy, consider adding a fresh angle on why the opportunity you're proposing is valuable when you follow up. Maybe it's a new sentence or just a few well-crafted words that capture a benefit you didn't mention in your original pitch. Offering not just a reminder but new information reiterates that you're enthusiastic about working with this person and gives him or her a new reason to consider your proposal.

Be polite, not pushy. We've been talking throughout this book about how you are not obligated to respond to anyone's email—unless, say, it's your boss and she can fire you. But remember that it goes both ways: Neither are you entitled to a response from someone else who, like you, might be too busy with their own tasks to deal with yours. This doesn't mean you shouldn't bother following up, but it does mean you should try to do it with grace and consideration. You might begin your message with, *I know*

ACTIVITY

Develop a system for keeping track of your pending items outside of your inbox.

If you're a paper person, I suggest making a list of your pending items on a Post-it that you place in a visible location near your desk. Next to each item make a note of your projected follow-up date. Then, as you make future to-do lists, you have a handy reminder in your line of sight. If you're a purely digital person, you can keep a separate pending list in your preferred task app, setting reminders (e.g., *follow up on invitation to Gretchen*, or *follow up on sales pitch to Ron*) to alert you to email them again on the appropriate date. Sure, this type of meticulous next-step sketching is anal, but that doesn't mean you should overlook it. Learning how to follow up with finesse is an essential part of getting shit done.

Dealing with Unwanted Inquiries

Email is an excellent medium for cold-calling people. (Learning how to do that well is, in fact, much of what the next section, Style, is about.) Of course, there's a flipside to this benefit: people are also going to be cold-calling you. And the more successful you become, the more unwanted inquiries you will receive.

That means your inbox is always going to be filled with a certain amount of emails in which people you don't know present you with "opportunities" or just straight up ask for your help. Just responding to these emails takes time, not to mention the hours committed if you actually agree to what's being asked. In other words, the crux of email management is largely about learning how to say no.

This is very difficult for some people, including myself. If you tend to be a people pleaser, it's hard to ignore genuine requests or turn folks away just because you are busy. Below are a few questions you can ask yourself to help clarify which emails are real opportunities and which are duds. Perhaps more importantly, they should also help you shift your mindset about who you do and do not owe a response.

Does this opportunity line up with your meaningful work goals? Earlier you outlined your meaningful work goals for the next three months, and they should come in very handy as you deal with the unsolicited inquiries in your inbox. You can simply measure each message against your goals and see if it serves them. Let's say one of those goals was to *enhance your public speaking ability,* and you've received an unexpected email invite to give a talk at a small conference. Great—respond and accept! What if it's an email asking you to write a guest blog post, but improving your writing is *not* one of your goals? In that case you politely decline. Every decision might not be so black-and-white, of course, but the point here is to develop a habit of weighing every email against your core priorities and then responding—or not—accordingly.

Is the email asking for something specific? If you're not careful, there's a certain type of email that can be a real time-suck: the unclear ask. Often well-intentioned people who admire something you've created or are interested in your expertise will write you an email asking you to hop on the phone and "explore synergies" or "brainstorm ideas." They obviously respect your work, which is flattering, yet what exactly they are asking for is unclear. If I'm intrigued, my policy for this type of email is to write back asking the person to clarify exactly what they want. If they're not willing to go the extra mile to specify their intent, they're probably just going to waste your time anyway. And if they do clarify, then you'll have a much better idea of what you're getting into.

Are they respecting your time, or is this a blind pitch?
The world is filled with people who want to pitch you their idea, their services, or their product. Assuming you didn't solicit the pitch, remember that you don't owe anyone in this category a response. Assess whether you were sent a template email: Did the person take the time to learn about you specifically and tailor their pitch? If they did and you're interested, that's worth responding to. If you're not interested, write them a concise no-thanks email if you have the bandwidth. And if they didn't take the time to do their homework before pitching you, rest easy knowing that you can consider the email spam and ignore it.

You must say "No" to unexpected opportunities

in order to say "Yes" to your priorities.

What if you're completely overwhelmed and don't have any extra time for random email inquiries? Occasionally you might be so overwhelmed that responding to unsolicited emails within a reasonable time frame—say, a week or two—is completely out of the question. If this is the situation, where you're just heads-down on a project and can't think about anything else for a month or two, I'd suggest crafting a short email template for declining unsolicited inquiries. Here's an example:

> *Hi Jackie—I appreciate your interest in my work. Unfortunately I'm 110% focused on an important creative project for the next few months and am unable to take on any additional work. But thank you for thinking of me!*

Having such templates handy takes the stress out of trying to craft a one-off email for every person who gets in touch. You can quickly decline with grace and stay focused on what's really important to you.

ACTIVITY

Let's experiment with applying Pareto's principle (or the 80-20 rule) to your unwanted inquiries.

It's likely that a small percentage of the people who send you email messages (say 20 percent) could be accounting for a massive amount of your wasted time (say 80 percent). Think about what types of unsolicited inquiries tend to really eat up your time. Maybe it's customers asking you the same questions again and again, or maybe it's aspiring writers who don't know how to give a good pitch. Once you identify what types of emails deliver the heaviest drag on your productivity, strategize about how to deal with them before they reach your inbox—whether that's setting up an auto-responder, using Gmail to create canned email responses, or redirecting them to an FAQ on your website.

PART THREE: STYLE

HOW TO WRITE EMAILS THAT PROVOKE ACTION

Let's face it: Every email is a pitch.

—Daniel Pink[20]

Don't Assume They're Paying Attention

If writing a letter a hundred years ago was the equivalent of sitting down with someone in a quiet room and talking face-to-face, writing an email today is like yelling at someone across a noisy traffic intersection while they're rushing to an appointment.

Everyone is overloaded and overbusy. We exist in a state of *continuous partial attention* as we shift nimbly back and forth between myriad forms of communication—email, text, instant message, social media, and the web.[21] That means your email isn't just competing with other email for someone's attention; it's competing with everything.

We're also reviewing our email on our mobile phones with increasing frequency. On average over 50 percent of emails are checked for the first time on a phone.[22] During that time we skim and trim our inboxes, responding to urgent items on the go and flagging less pressing items to be revisited when we're back at our desks.

That means your email will most likely be digested in a quick glance while the receiver is on their phone, flitting back and forth between other tasks. At best your correspondence will get a quick flash of their attention. If it's deemed compelling based on that passing glance, they will probably return to it later. But if you make a poor first impression, it's game over before you even get started.

This competition for attention means we now have to approach things very differently in terms of composing. In this section on style, I'll outline how to write effective emails in a world where everyone is busy and attention is scarce. We'll start with the importance of considering your audience and then move onto a series of tips for tailoring your emails to be concise, actionable, and personable.

What I won't be going into detail about is what form of greeting and sign-off you should use. Depending on where in the world you are, the customs will be different. In my examples and scripts throughout the remainder of the book, I use a style that's common in the US, but you should feel free to substitute the greetings and sign-offs that feel right for your culture.

Considering Your Audience

We typically write emails in a bubble. We compose alone and without feedback. This can make it feel like a private, personal act when in fact it's not about you at all. It's about the two of you. Every email is a conversation, a social interaction that requires politeness, sensitivity, finesse, and kindness.

Which is why your most important task before composing an email is to *consider your audience*. Are you writing to your boss? To an important person you don't know? To a client or customer who might be upset? To a coworker who's on the verge of burnout? Each of these scenarios demand different writing strategies and tones. Rather than focusing on what you need, put yourself in their shoes: How busy are they? What information do they need? What would put them at ease?

If this sounds like a lot of work for a little old email, think about it this way: if you take the time to consider your audience and their needs now, your emails will be more effective, you will be more likely to get what you want, you will have fewer fires to put out, and you will ultimately have to spend less time on email.

Being Concise & Actionable

Inside each of us there is a little efficiency guru who views every single email within a larger matrix of all the stuff we could be focusing on—the big deadline that needs to be met, the presentation that needs to be prepared, the client conflict that needs to be resolved, the errands that need to be run. I call this the *busy bias*, and it colors how much—or how little—attention we are willing to give any one interaction or piece of information.

When everyone is busy, a key part of getting people to pay attention is being respectful of their time. In the context of composing email this means being clear, concise, and actionable. You can achieve this by sticking to a few simple strategies for structuring the information you need to communicate:

Lead with the ask. Without being abrupt or pushy, it's important to put your ask at the top of your email—within the first sentence or two if possible. The goal is to get the reader's attention and have them understand the action that's being requested immediately. If you put a lot of rigmarole before your ask, an impatient reader might never get to it. For example, let's say you're reaching out to the CEO of a startup you admire to invite her to speak at a conference. You could position the ask like so:

Hi Catherine—This is Mark Holland. I run the popular Firestarters conference, which draws over 5,000 entrepreneurs to the Staples Center in LA each year. I'm writing to extend an invitation for you to speak at our event on March 5th, 2016.

Catherine may not know what the hell the Firestarters conference is yet, but she does know something important: *What this email is about* (a speaking invitation). She also now knows the date and location of the event and that it has fairly impressive attendance numbers. Now that the ask is clear and her interest is piqued, Mark can go on to give her some backstory on the event, share more impressive stats, and make his case even stronger.

In a short-attention span world, it's best to get right to the point immediately and do your explaining later. Think about what will appear in the two-line message preview the recipient will see as she scrolls through her inbox: Will it capture her attention?

Attention doesn't come for free anymore.
You must command it.

Establish your credibility. *Why should I care?* is the tacit question hovering in most people's minds as they open an email, especially if it's from someone they don't know. This is why establishing your credibility early on in the message is crucial. Tell your reader why you are different, why you are accomplished, or why they should pay attention to you.

For instance, if you're cold-emailing a brand to request a sponsorship, you might establish your credibility by sharing data points about your audience and the awards you've won.

> *Hi Tom—I'm Tracy Black, the editor of Feed Daily, a Webby award–winning website with over 2 million visitors a month. I'm putting together a new article series that targets ambitious young creatives, and I wanted to see if you might be interested in sponsoring it?*

If you're emailing someone you do know—getting in touch with a coworker about an urgent task, for example— you might legitimize your request by indicating that you are under pressure from the boss (assuming that's true).

Hi Tom—I'm following up to see if you were able to implement the new email signup feature? The CEO wants to see this wrapped up by the end of the week.

But data points and brute authority aren't your only options, of course. You can also establish credibility by being a keen observer of the person you are contacting: you could tell them how long you've followed their work, what you enjoyed about the last blog post they wrote, or how their product might be improved—with tact of course! As long as it's not fawning, most people appreciate being noticed—and it makes them notice you back.

Make the way forward clear. You're much more likely to get a response from someone if it's clear what the next step is. I frequently receive emails from people who are interested in some sort of knowledge exchange but never clarify how they would like for me to take action. Do they want to have a coffee? Do they want to do a phone call? It's unclear, which means that instead of saying, "Yes!" I have to respond by asking them what they're asking me for in the first place—or, more likely, not respond at all. By making the way forward clear, you make it easy for the recipient to say yes to your request.

Let's say you're reaching out to a film director you admire for advice. Don't just email them with:

I've been a fan of your work for years, and I'd love to pick your brain. What do you say?

Instead, propose something specific:

I'm a longtime admirer of your work and have the greatest respect for your filmmaking expertise. I would love to ask you a few questions about how you financed your first film. Would you be game for a 15-20 minute phone call next week? My schedule is wide open all day Thursday and Friday if you have availability then. I promise to keep it brief.

The second example clarifies the subject matter at hand and the fact that you just want to do a brief phone call. This means that the recipient knows the time commitment will be minimal and—because you've already proposed a calendar date—they know that the email thread can be closed quickly and efficiently. In other words, you've respected their time, and they now know that dealing with you won't be another headache they don't need.

If you're asking a question, propose a solution. Email is not a good venue for debate. Thus, messages that offer nothing but a question like—*What do you think about X?*—are generally ineffectual. Busy people don't want to figure out your problems for you, and they don't want to write you a lengthy response. They want to say yes or no and then move on to the next thing. So if you want to get a response—and to get your way—don't just pose questions; propose solutions.

Let's imagine that you're emailing your boss to ask if you can attend a conference. You could write,

> *Hi Tina—I noticed that people are already booking hotels for the SXSW conference next year. I'd like to go. What do you think?*

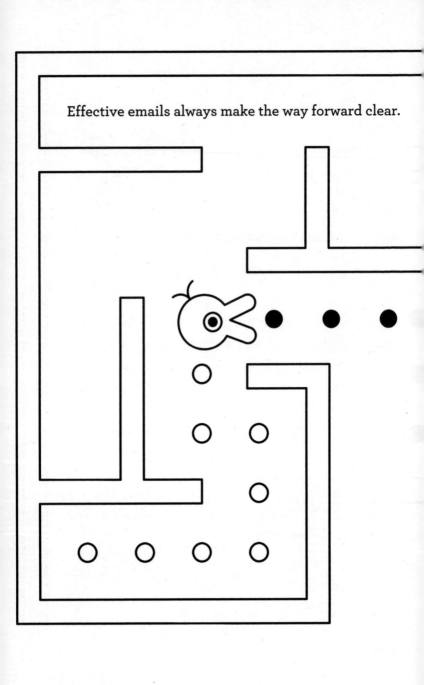

Effective emails always make the way forward clear.

Or, you could write,

> *Hi Tina—I've been thinking about ways to enrich my work skill set, and it looks like there are some speakers and workshops at SXSW next year that would be very helpful. I can also put together a report to share what I've learned with the team after I return. I've estimated the cost, and it looks like a ticket, hotel, and airfare would run the company about $2,500. Do you think the company could sponsor me to attend?*

The first message is short but lazy and will require numerous back-and-forth messages to clarify what's really at stake. The second email is longer but includes everything necessary for the conversation to be resolved immediately. The writer has done her homework, the costs and benefits are clear, and it's easy for the boss to just say yes. Being proactive in your communications takes more work upfront, but it pays huge dividends in the long run.

Be scannable. Use bullets, numbers, and/or bolding to make your email skimmable and digestible, emphasizing the key points. If you scoff at this type of spoon-feeding of information, go ahead and get over it. Emails are about getting results, not testing your recipient's reading comprehension. Here's an example of how you might recap next steps after a client meeting.

Hi Sharon—Great call yesterday! I'm excited about next steps. Here's a recap of what we discussed doing in the coming week to meet our deadline:

Action Items for Sharon & Team:
- *Approve revised mockups (Due: Mon 4/9)*
- *Provide final copy for banners (Due: Wed 4/11)*
- *Supply hi-res photography (Due: Wed 4/11)*

Because this email requires the client to do something, you want the action items to pop out of the email—thus the bold text—and be easily digested—thus the bullets. Due dates are also offset in parentheses so they're easy to see. Remember: if you really want to get things done, success depends upon making it easy for your reader to quickly process the email and understand the salient points.

Give them a deadline. Is your email urgent? Does it need a response now? In two days? In two weeks? It may surprise you to learn that busy people love deadlines because they help prioritize exactly when things need to get done. In fact, I've found that emails that have no timetable are more likely to get ignored. You certainly don't want to be imperious or overly demanding, but do give your reader some polite context for timing.

If you're emailing a close colleague about an urgent task, you can be pretty straightforward about timing:

For the project to stay on schedule, I'll need a response from you in the next 24 hours if possible.

If you're extending an invitation to someone you haven't met, you might politely share your follow-up timeline:

I'm sure you're busy and will want time to mull this opportunity over. I'll follow up in two weeks if I haven't heard from you.

Or say you want to allow your boss or a client to weigh in on a decision but need to move forward if they don't respond in time:

> *If I don't hear back from you by this Friday, Aug 17th, I'll go ahead and proceed with the solution I've proposed above.*

Including a deadline is like dropping an anchor: it fixes your request in space and time, making it more likely to get noticed and get done.

Write your subject lines like headlines. For your email to be read, it has to be opened. Your goal should be to compose a subject line that is clear and, ideally, provocative. It's much like writing a compelling headline for an article or blog post that you want people to click on. Let's say you're a successful musician reaching out to a designer about doing the cover for your new record. You have a decent-sized audience, so you expect the album to perform well. You could use:

> *Subject: Design Gig*

Imagine you are the Oscar Wilde of email.
Be pithy.

It's accurate, but it lacks specificity and makes your email sound like a humdrum offer. Alternatively you could use:

Subject: Cover design for high-profile album release?

This is still accurate, but it piques curiosity by clarifying what exactly the project is and promising good exposure. Especially when you're writing an "ask" email to someone you've never met before, the subject line functions like a first impression. And you only get one chance to make a first impression.

Edit your messages ruthlessly. After you've drafted your email, re-examine it with an unsympathetic eye and take out anything unnecessary. Being clear and concise from the get-go saves time for everyone. (Of course, you want to achieve this without seeming abrupt, but more on being friendly in the next section.) There's no doubt it takes more time to craft a tight and to-the-point email, but it will also be much more likely to get a response.

Preview all messages on your phone. As mentioned earlier, your email message is most likely going to be opened first on a mobile phone. Therefore, it's wise to understand what your message will look like on a handheld. What seems digestible on a massive desktop screen often looks like *War and Peace* on a mobile phone. Preview your message on the small screen, and if it still looks way too long, ruthlessly edit it again. If your message gives the impression of being overwhelming, it's probably going to get ignored.

Style Checklist

☐ Be scannable.

☐ Lead with the ask.

☐ Establish your credibility.

☐ Make the way forward clear.

☐ Give them a deadline.

☐ If you're asking a question, propose a solution.

☐ Write your subject lines like headlines.

☐ Preview all messages on your phone.

☐ Edit ruthlessly.

Being Friendly & Persuasive

With every email you write you are essentially combating two forms of bias. We just talked about the first one: the *busy bias*. The second, more insidious bias is the *negativity bias*, which I discussed earlier (see page 17). To quickly recap: research has shown that when we receive an email, we are predisposed to view the tone of that message negatively, or at least more negatively than the sender views the tone of their message.

Given that everyone has this natural negativity bias against email, it's important to pay close attention to your phrasing. For the most part we use email either to remind people about things they said they would do or to ask them to do something for us. In the absence of social cues, this is a delicate task.

What's more, you are also presumably building relationships with people as you communicate, and it's beneficial if you seem likable. Which is all to say: While being concise and respectful of people's time is extremely important, it is equally important to be friendly and respectful of them as human beings. A few tips for making your emails personable:

Do not use the imperative. If you've forgotten your grammar lessons, the imperative is the mood I just used in that bolded sentence. It is essentially a command: *do this, go there, finish that.* In general you want to avoid using the imperative in email. People like to feel they have agency in their work, and the imperative turns them into peons following orders. (And if you're speaking to someone above you, it sounds downright presumptuous.)

Rather than using the imperative, try to make a habit of using the conditional—*Could you? Would you?*—when asking someone to do a task. Instead of saying *do this*, ask them *if they could do this*. It's a subtle shift in phrasing, but it conveys a big shift in perspective: you're putting the ball in their court and respecting their right to make decisions about what they will do and when.

Emphasize the benefits of the task. If you're sending an email to someone, you probably have a good reason why—that is, there's some benefit to you. But what's in it for them? People like to have a reason for doing things. If you want to get a positive reaction to your message, it's helpful to provide some greater context for the request. The "why," if you will.

You could frame the benefit in terms of quality:

I know this is frustrating, but it will make the product even better.

Or in terms of progression:

We're so close to meeting the deadline; we'll be just about there after this one last push.

Or even in terms of gratitude:

If you could just make this one tweak, it would really help me out, and then we'll be done.

Provide context and communicate progress. As you no doubt noticed in the previous examples, I chose to emphasize the fact that the task was "almost done" in multiple instances. The human brain likes to feel a sense of completion, as we covered earlier in the book; people are always more motivated when the end is in sight. Even if you're not near the end of a project, framing a request in terms of completing a milestone or some other small step can be helpful. The happy sense of completion could even come from the promise of not getting any more email from you, such as:

Once you wrap up this task, I can take over the next stage of the project, and you won't have to get all these emails from me anymore!

The point is to put the request on a timeline and show progress so your recipient understands, *If I do this, we will be moving forward.*

Acknowledge their workload. A little consideration goes a long way. I've found that people are much more receptive to requests if you take the time to acknowledge that you recognize they're busy, as in:

I know you have a really hectic schedule, but let me quickly explain why I think this opportunity is worth your while...

Or you can close an email with:

Motivation, and swift replies, come from understanding WHY.

Thanks for taking time out of your no doubt busy schedule to consider my request.

By empathizing with their workload, you cut off the possibility of a *They think I have time for this?!* type of reaction to your email, and communicate to them that you understand the context of your request. Explicitly indicating that you are aware of—and respect—other people's time is always a good idea.

Make it personal. People like to feel that they have a unique contribution to make. If your email is an ask and/or a cold call, tell the recipient why you've chosen to reach out to them *in particular*. When I curated speakers for a popular creative conference, I would always mention something I admired about the prospective speaker's work and what I thought they might give a talk about in my outreach emails, such as:

I've been following your research on vulnerability and courage closely for years. I'm particularly interested in the findings in your new book and am wondering if you could give a talk about how vulnerability impacts artists and their creative process?

This type of specificity makes it clear that you have been genuinely thoughtful about their work and how it might be integrated into the opportunity you are proposing. If you're asking an individual to participate in something, ostensibly you are interested in them—show it.

Earnestness and enthusiasm are underrated. Email is the last place you want to play it cool. In fact, it's hard to go wrong if you always focus on conveying a super-positive, hardworking attitude in every message you write. You might think you sound overly earnest or even chirpy when you read back your email, but remember that the negativity bias will immediately take the language down a notch when it hits that person's inbox. I used to be staunchly against exclamation points and emoticons, but I changed my tune as soon as I had to manage a bunch of moody creatives via email. Upbeat punctuation makes your enthusiasm and support palpable to the reader, supplying the social cues that are generally absent. And so

Empathy isn't a nice-to-have, it's a necessity.

what if you sound like a cheerleader—couldn't we all use a little more support at work?

Terseness is earned. You have probably received emails from very successful and busy people that were extremely terse. Perhaps it was from your boss or from a successful entrepreneur or investor. Regardless, do not take these emails as cues for how *you* should write emails. With power and renown come benefits, and one of those benefits, in some people's minds, is the chance to not mince words. It works for them because in most instances the people they are emailing have no choice but to accept their curt style of communication. It does not mean such an approach is advisable for you or for anyone who values kindness and consideration.

Express gratitude. Research has shown that people are more likely to help you—and others—in the future if you say thank you.[23] Whether you're writing to a coworker about meeting a deadline or you're asking someone you've never met to help you out, a little gratitude goes a long way. Thank them for their efforts, thank them for considering your request, and thank them for devoting a small amount of their valuable time and energy to your email. Appreciation is a much more effective motivator than obligation.

* * *

All of that said, I know that the world is made of more than sunshine and giggles, and sometimes friendliness just doesn't get the job done. Although I always recommend a can-do attitude, good cheer, and gratitude as your de facto email approach, certain circumstances demand a firmer hand. When dire straits arrive—or, better yet, *before* they arrive—you can consult the special Cheat Sheets section at the back of this book for tactful advice on everything from delivering criticism and rejecting applications or pitches to responding to angry customers and getting clients to pay you. Surprisingly, most of these things can be accomplished with relative ease—and kindness—if you choose your words wisely.

Style Checklist

- [ ] Don't use the imperative (oops).

- [ ] Avoid overly terse, unfeeling replies.

- [ ] Emphasize the benefits of the task.

- [ ] Provide context, and communicate progress.

- [ ] Express enthusiasm and earnestness.

- [ ] Make them feel unique and special.

- [ ] Acknowledge their workload.

- [ ] Be thankful!

Not Being an Idiot

The lowest level of email etiquette is not screwing up. Details matter, and a misspelled name or a grammatically off sentence can easily get you dismissed from someone's inbox. Though small, such errors come off as inattentive and unprofessional. They make it easy for people not to pay attention to you.

Then there's the next order of error, which can truly sabotage a relationship: those moments when you accidentally forward a message to the wrong person or write an ill-advised email because you're grumpy or tired. Then someone blows up, and you spend the rest of the day fretting and doing damage control.

Below are a few rules, many of which I learned the hard way, that will help you stay in the good graces of everyone you email and avoid messy fallouts.

Consider: Should this even be an email? Yes, I mentioned this earlier in the book, but it's so important, I'm saying it again. Emailing effectively is about responding consciously and considerately. Just because someone contacted you via email does not mean you need to respond via email. Consider what you're trying to accomplish first. Email is great for scheduling, brief updates and requests, reaching out to people you don't know, and one-way communication with large groups. But email is wretched for things like debating business priorities, delivering delicate feedback, discussing problems with lots of small details, or making complex decisions involving many people. If you don't think email is the best means for responding, trust your instincts and choose a better approach.

Ask people to "opt-in" before you introduce them. Email is frequently used for introductions. Maybe you know someone to whom I want to pitch an idea, so I ask you to help me out with an introduction. But what about the other person? Do they want the introduction? Maybe they're heads-down on a creative project, or maybe they're overwhelmed and have absolutely no time to listen to new pitches—you don't know until you ask. That's why it's always a good idea to make sure both parties opt in before the introduction is made. Checking with the other person before you make an intro ensures you won't be putting them in an awkward position by providing them with yet another unwanted inquiry. It also ensures you won't be unwittingly sabotaging your relationship with them.

Type in your recipient's email address only after your draft is complete. This seems counterintuitive—we typically start an email by typing in the address of the person we're writing to. Unfortunately this makes it really easy, with one accidental click, to send a message before you're ready to. Especially if you're crafting a complex email, this can give the person you're writing to an unwanted peek behind the scenes of your thought process. Or it can result in them receiving a truncated message, which looks unprofessional. Putting in the address after you're happy with the draft ensures it's impossible to send the email too early and embarrass yourself.

Proactively prune your email threads. Part of respecting other people's time is trying to remove information clutter whenever possible. That means rather than just *Replying All*, you should be constantly pruning the CCs on all of your messages. Only CC essential actors on any given email thread, and remove anyone who is superfluous. The polite way to remove someone from a thread is to shift them from CC to BCC, saying, *I'm moving Andy to bcc*, at the beginning of the message. Then Andy won't get any future replies to the thread, but he will also know that he was consciously removed rather than thinking someone dropped the ball. And if he has a problem with being removed from the thread, he has the opportunity to say so.

Don't email when you're angry, hungry, or tired. If you work a lot, you are probably in one of the aforementioned states quite often. It's tempting to email in this condition, especially when you're angry. But you will always— *always*—regret it. Instead of sending an email when you're in the wrong state of mind, make a compromise: go ahead and draft the email—without inputting the email address, as above—and get those feelings off your chest. Then calm down, eat something, or take a nap. Once you're feeling more stable—ideally, the following day—review the draft and see if you still want to send it. Hopefully you don't. Email is a terrible medium for confrontation, so if you absolutely have to let off some stream, try doing it in person or on the phone if you can. Then at least the social

When in doubt, take a moment to collect your thoughts.
Urgency is the root of all idiocy.

feedback loop will be present and you're less likely to make a total hash of it.

Never escalate on email. Even if you're striving to be mindful, you will still make mistakes from time to time. So what happens when you accidentally send someone a crappy email that your better self regrets moments later? If the recipient hasn't replied yet, go ahead and send a follow-up email acknowledging your error and clarifying with a more positive message. You can start with:

I was in a rush when I sent my previous email, and I struck the wrong tone. What I meant to say was . . .

When you do this, make sure to forward your original email with your new, more emotionally intelligent message on top so it stays on the same conversation thread. (That way the recipient will see the improved email first if he hasn't read the original already.) If the recipient has already replied to your message and is as hurt or huffy as you expected, then immediately take the conversation offline. If you're in the same office, go find him at his desk. If you're in different locations, then give him a call. Once a conversation goes south on email, it can rarely be repaired there.

Don't write anything you wouldn't say to someone's face. I don't mean don't write something to Derek that you wouldn't say to Derek's face; I mean don't write something to Sarah *about Derek* that you wouldn't say to Derek's face. An email is a record, and it doesn't disappear after you send it. It's good practice to assume that anything you write could eventually be forwarded onto someone else. Perhaps even the person you are talking about. So if you need to have a bitch session, do it offline.

Don't reply to forwarded emails. This is related to not talking trash in email, but slightly different. For example, let's say your coworker forwards you a customer service inquiry that you need to respond to. When they forward it to you, they make a snarky comment about how dumb the customer's question is. When you respond to the email, you hit *Reply*, swap in the customer's email, and plan to cut out your coworker's comment. But unfortunately you forget to remove that part of the email thread before you send the message. Now the customer can see the whole thread, including your coworker's comment, and you look like jerks.

To avoid this type of snafu, make a habit of never replying to forwarded messages. Instead, open up a new message, paste in the part of the forwarded thread that you need, and type your response above it. This procedure makes it fairly difficult to screw up in the way I just described. Additionally, as a matter of good etiquette, don't write anything about the original sender that you would not like for them to read when you forward a message to someone else for response.

Be as nice as possible. Always. This final point has been more or less implicit in all of the preceding tips, but it's worth reiterating. Being a jerk in email is never worth the steam you let off in the process. Any unkind words you type almost always come back on you or, worse, create some type of damage-control situation that eats up hours of your time and drains you of energy. In other words, if you're not motivated to be nice because of the good karma, be motivated to be nice because ultimately it saves time.

Style Checklist

☐ Ask: Is email the right medium for this message?

☐ Avoid hitting Send if you're hungry, angry, or tired. (Seriously.)

☐ Never escalate a misunderstanding on email.

☐ Have people opt in before you introduce them.

☐ Draft first, add email addresses last.

☐ Move to BCC proactively.

☐ Don't talk trash.

PART FOUR: SUPERPOWERS

HOW TO USE YOUR NEW ARSENAL OF EMAIL SKILLS TO CONQUER SOCIAL MEDIA, TECHNOLOGY, AND OTHER DISTRACTIONS

Creation is in part merely the business of forgoing the great and small distractions.

—E. B. White[24]

Why Email Is the Ultimate Pop Quiz

There is an old saying: *Tools make excellent servants, but very poor masters.* This is especially true when it comes to technology. One of the skills that will make or break all of us in the twenty-first century is the ability to try out and master new technologies.

Amazingly, email has been around for 25+ years now, and it's still wreaking havoc on our lives. This is partly because advances in how and where we can receive email keep changing the game. Got a system figured out for when your email is only accessible at work? How about we give you email on a mobile phone and see how that goes? Now you've got it figured out on your phone? How about we notify you of every new email message via your wristwatch? And so on. You get the idea.

Far from being unique, email is just one example of how a new technology can rapidly become a central actor in life as we know it. The rise of smartphones, text messaging, and social media have each had an equally seismic impact on how we live and how we work: smartphones made location obsolete, text messages made talking obsolete, and social media made privacy obsolete.

These types of massive paradigm shifts are not going to stop. As new technologies come online we will be required to reconsider our relationship to existing technologies. What's more, we will be asked to consider afresh how we spend our time and how we focus our attention.

Ten years ago we spent zero time on social media because it didn't exist. Now we spend an average of 1.72 hours a day on social media alone and a whopping 6+ hours a day online.[25] But what are we sacrificing? What would we have done with all of those hours ten years ago?

In essence every new technology acts like a pop quiz for our priorities, offering new delights and distractions that compete for our attention. The upside is that we are never at a loss for something to entertain or absorb our minds. The downside is a corrosive, minute-to-minute brand of choice anxiety that requires us to constantly make decisions about when, where, and how much attention we give an item, app, or task. We must decide, over and over again, which activities are worthy of our concerted focus and which are unproductive distractions.

These are, of course, exactly the issues we have wrestled with throughout this book, specifically through the lens of email. But the lessons learned can be applied far beyond. Because, at its core, all of the advice I have [of]fered here is about how to communicate and how to man-age your attention in an era of information overload.

The reasons why email makes us crazy, as outlined in the first section of this book, also apply to numerous other technologies. Social media, text messaging, and real-time chat programs are all addictive random rewards systems that stimulate our rat brains. Twitter, Facebook, Slack, and the like all offer streams of information that are alternately delightful, insightful, aggravating, and mind-numbing. But what they never are is predictable. Each of these medi-ums, like email, offers a powerfully attractive lever that we can pull to escape the less sexy—and sustained—demands of doing meaningful work. But if we want to achieve some-thing of value, we must master the art of tuning them out when it's time to focus on more pressing priorities.

Similarly, the negativity bias influences our perception of any electronic message we type, not just emails. You can flame out after texting someone a poorly phrased message on your phone, or you can post an ill-considered tweet that incites a furor of replies because people did not take it as you intended. Even in electronic mediums that are seemingly more instant, the crippling powers of the

...gativity bias still apply. As our interactions with family, ...nds, and coworkers are increasingly mediated by technologies that shortcut the traditional social cues of facial ...ession, vocal tone, and physical gesture, we must ...ke an even greater effort to explicitly convey our empathy and enthusiasm to combat a baseline negative reaction. How surprising to learn that living in a digital world demands more sensitivity and subtlety than any of us expected.

What's more, as we leave a world of tangible, physical communication—newspapers, letters, bills—far behind in favor of all-digital communication, we shift from a state where incoming information was limited by physical space—whatever could, literally, fit in your mailbox—to a state where the amount of incoming information you can receive is utterly unlimited. In other words, what's incoming—other people's updates, inquiries, and offers—will now always exceed what's outgoing—what we're actually capable of responding to. You could easily fritter away your whole day commenting on every Facebook update your friends post or responding to every @ reply you receive on Twitter. An unlimited stream of information awaits at all times, willing to eat up as much of your time and energy as you want to give it. But if you give all of your attention to inputs from other people, you will have nothing left with which to create your own outputs.

That's why the strategies outlined in the second section of this book—methodically outlining your goals, defining a daily routine, and setting expectations with yourself and others for how and when you will communicate—are so essential. It's not just about email; it's about learning how to manage your attention more effectively with regard to any—and every—distracting input or interruption that comes your way. Success has always gone to those who could apply their talents in a single-minded manner over an extended period of time to achieve a given outcome. As a surfeit of new apps and communication channels come online and bid for our precious attention, this will only become more true. Having the wherewithal—and the willpower—to set priorities, stay the course, and ignore irrelevant "opportunities" is a skill that's second to none in this cacophonous and demanding digital age.

On the flipside, now that we live in a world where attention is scarce, understanding how to command attention—and get people to take action—is one of our greatest challenges. As we begin to communicate significantly more through the written word than face-to-face interaction, writing well has become a core skill everyone must cultivate. Increasingly we are judged—and applauded or dismissed—based on our words alone. A prospective employer might scan the text on your LinkedIn profile or personal blog and make a snap judgment about who you are. The promotional copy you write for your app, book, or Kickstarter project will determine whether people want to buy what you're selling. The pitch email you write to a VC will determine whether you ever land a meeting to talk about funding for your startup.

In this landscape the style tips in the third section of this book are relevant not just to writing email but to writing in general. If you want people to pay attention to you, your ideas, and your creations, you need to be able to craft language that cuts through the noise. Those who can grasp that we are all busy and distracted and can write concise, compelling prose that gets people to pay attention *despite their scatterbrained state* will be more successful than those who can't.

At the end of the day, being good at email is not a single skill. It is a collection of skills—the ability to prioritize and execute, to be empathetic and affable, to express yourself clearly and concisely—that applies to nearly all aspects of work and life. Beyond that, observing how you deal with email is an excellent object lesson in understanding how you will deal with this young century's greatest challenge: distraction.

* * *

I wrote a book about email—and how to repair our relationship with it—because I believe that email is the single biggest distraction that plagues us at work. Distraction is the enemy of creativity. It deadens our ability to accomplish anything of import. And worse, it lulls us into a feeling of engagement, of busyness, that feels productive even as it destroys any possibility of meaningful productivity.

If we let our lives be run by endless inputs—by pings and buzzes and status updates and moments—we will never create anything of value. We make great things when we exert our unwavering attention over time on completing a single task. Value simply cannot be created in an instant, nor can it be created in tiny little five- to ten-minute bursts of focus in between checking your Twitter feed. Value emerges as the product of focused work that unfolds over time. As Lewis Hyde wrote in his beautiful book about creativity, *The Gift*: "There is no technology, no time-saving device that can alter the rhythms of creative labor."[26]

No matter how strong the allure of technology, we must not let it take away our ability to attend, to quite literally train our attention on a given task and keep it there. Because all meaningful work, all creative acts, emerge from our ability to focus the ultimate technology, the human mind, on realizing a single goal. Whether you're having a spirited debate with a colleague, writing a thoughtful blog post, or building a small business from the ground up, all of these acts, small and large, depend upon your ability to attend, to care, to invest your time and energy into one thing to the exclusion of all others. Craft, empathy, conviction—these values are not the hallmarks of a distracted person. They are the province of the focused mind.

Email is but one—admittedly great—distraction among many we currently face, some of which already exist—Twitter, Facebook, Instagram, Slack, Snapchat—and many which have yet to be invented. But email is probably the best test that exists today of your ability to marshal your attention away from unproductive distractions and onto the meaningful work that truly matters to you. If you can learn to master your email, you will have gone a long way toward solving the existential problem at the heart of technology in the Internet Age: overcoming distraction and its many discontents.

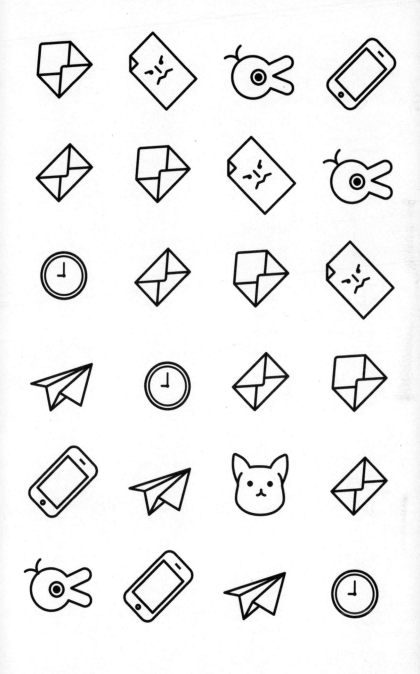

CHEAT SHEETS

PRESCRIPTIONS FOR COMMON EMAIL PROBLEMS

[APPLY AS NEEDED]

EVERYDAY EMAIL SCRIPTS

Advanced Email Scripts

EVERYDAY
EMAIL
SCRIPTS

Crafting an Email Signature

Ever gotten an email where the signature was ten times longer than the message? Not classy. In the mobile era it's wise to avoid a bloated email signature. The only real essentials are your title and contact info. A street address is optional and should be included only if people regularly send you mail or visit your office. Things not to include: inspirational quotes (which get tired after the first email exchange), images or logos (which look like false document attachments to your recipient), your email address (it's in the "from" field!), or 17 promotional links to your website, Twitter, Instagram, TEDx talk, podcast, and more.

Think about the impression you want to give and include only the items that are relevant. If you're a photographer, sharing your Instagram makes sense. If you're a book reviewer, links to your article feed and a mailing address for review copies makes sense. If you're building up a mailing list, a link to your newsletter signup makes sense. As Thoreau said, "Simplify, ~~simplify~~." A few samples:

Jocelyn K. Glei
jkglei.com/newsletter
@jkglei

Tom James
Director, Startup.ly
707-543-1234

Kristin Court
Photo Journalist
Website: kristincourt.com
Instagram: @courtie

Jim Thirwell
Senior Critic, NYRB
Call: 212-345-6789
Read: nyrb.com/thirwell
Mail: 805 Broadway, NYC, 10001

Composing an Out-of-Office Message

The key to writing a successful out-of-office message is to not overpromise. Just be straight with people: tell them when you're gone, when you'll be back at your desk, and when you'll get to their message. An example:

Hi there—I'm out of the office from Monday Nov 11– Friday Nov 15. I will not be responding to any emails during my vacation.

I will be back at my desk on Monday Nov 18th and will respond to your email as soon as possible. I will likely have a backlog, so I appreciate your patience.

It's better to set low expectations and exceed them than to set high expectations and fail. (To be clear: this is not a recommended mantra for life, just out-of-office messages.) Even if you might check your email during vacation, it's better to say you won't. Then when you're lying on the beach, thinking, *There is no way in hell I'm checking my work email,* you won't be letting anyone down. And if you do decide to respond while you're away, it's a pleasant surprise.

Curbing Unproductive Brainstorming

When you're on an email thread with a large group, the "What if?" conversations can really start to spiral out of control, distracting you and clogging up your inbox. What's more, all those ideas will probably get lost in the shuffle because email is such a terrible medium for brainstorming. The best strategy here is to politely nip the idea sharing in the bud by proposing a better place to brainstorm, such as,

> *Guys—So many good ideas on this thread! How about we take the conversation offline so that we can talk it through more thoroughly? Can everyone do a meeting this Thursday 4/15 at 3pm?*

> *I've captured all the ideas so far in this Google doc: [link]. Moving forward, let's put additional thoughts in here, and then we'll use the doc to guide the meeting agenda.*

If you don't use Google Docs, there are numerous other services that allow you to share and edit documents as a group. That way you can keep track of everyone's ideas in one place without spamming anyone's inbox.

Getting Off Annoying Email Threads

It sucks when you're stuck on an email thread of declining relevance. You have nothing to add, but you can't escape. There are a few options for solving this quandary. If you don't know anyone on the thread very well, you must ask the group to remove you. The most elegant approach here is to indicate that everyone is doing such a great job talking among themselves that you are now superfluous.

> *Looks like you guys have taken the reins on this conversation! Would you mind moving me to "bcc" so that I can bow out?*

However, if you have a close colleague or friend on the thread, you can reply *only to them* with a more honest message, asking to be moved to BCC:

> *Sean—Would you mind moving me to "bcc" when you respond? I'm waging war on inbox clutter this week. ;)*

If you can, directing your request for removal to a specific person makes it more likely to get done. That said, if both of these approaches are unsuitable, there is a third way.

If you use Gmail, you can find a magical Mute option under the More menu on your inbox screen. When you apply the mute button, all further conversation on the thread automatically skips your inbox and is archived. If you want to check up on the conversation later, you can search on Is:muted. This function also works well for hiding forum threads gone wild and other automatic notifications that contribute to inbox clutter.

Following Up After a Productive Meeting

The failure of most meetings comes after the event. You get together and discuss some earth-shattering ideas, but then no one follows up about next steps and nothing really happens. If you're truly committed to getting shit done and looking like an ace professional, take it upon yourself to quickly recap next steps within 24 hours of every meeting you have. When you follow up include agreed-upon due dates, start each task with an active verb, and segment tasks out by who's doing what. Here's how you might follow up after an internal meeting:

Guys—Great meeting yesterday afternoon! Here's what we all agreed to accomplish by Fri 6/13.

Dave:
—Fix email signup form bug

Jessica:
—Code new email newsletter design for mobile
—Send test emails to team by Thur afternoon

Emily:
—Finalize email subject line
—Merge emails lists as discussed

It's also a good idea to follow up after informal meetings when appropriate.

Hi Carla—Great to chat with you today!

Here's the article I mentioned about how conversations suffer when a cell phone is on the table: [Link]

I'll introduce you to the prospective intern I mentioned as soon as I hear back from him.

You can find another example for following up after a client meeting on page 113.

Asking Your Boss for Things

Maybe you need time off, maybe you want to attend a conference, or maybe you want to hire more staff. Whatever you're asking for, make sure you frame the request in terms of the value it provides to your boss and/or the company rather than the value it provides to you. You'll also want to make it clear that you've thought through any eventualities stemming from the request and have them covered. A new-hire request might look like this:

Hi Karen—I know you're about to set budgets for the coming year, and I wanted to ask if we could discuss the possibility of hiring a new salesperson? I've looked at the numbers, and adding someone should allow us to double the new accounts we bring in each year, which means it should only take about three months for the new hire to pay for his salary in value added to the company.

While a vacation request might look like this:

Hi Karen—I wanted to request your approval on taking some vacation in October: Mon 10/6 thru Mon 10/13. We'll have just wrapped the big web relaunch, so it'll be a slow period, and Mark has agreed to step in and handle all my clients during my absence. Then I can come back rested and refreshed for the big holiday sales push!

On page 112 you can find a sample script for asking your boss if you can attend a conference. Whatever the request, remember the cardinal rule of asking: make it easy to say yes.

Setting Up a Meeting with Someone You Admire

One of the great wonders of the Internet is the relative ease with which you can get in touch with almost anyone. But that doesn't mean the person you're reaching out to owes you anything. Rather than feeling entitled to a reply, consider an email to someone you admire like a brief audition for their attention. Introduce yourself, establish your credibility, and display knowledge of their work. If the person is of a similar level of professional accomplishment to you, recommending a coffee meeting is fine.

> *Hi Robin—Kevin Coates, freelance journalist here. I've been following your writing about the future of work on your blog and in* Wired *magazine for years now. I myself write a weekly newsletter on the changing career landscape called* Free Agents *that has 20,000+ subscribers. I'm wondering if you'd be game to grab a quick coffee sometime to talk shop?*

If they're way out of your league, then suggest a quick phone call instead.

Hi Michael—C. K. Chalmers, college student here. Your recent videos for Bjork and Aphex Twin are lightyears ahead of anything else I've seen recently. I'm currently studying film at NYU with the intention of becoming a music video director. I'm writing to inquire if you would be willing to do a 15–20 minute phone call with me to discuss your digital animation techniques?

I know it's a big ask, but I want to learn from the best of the best. I'm sure you're very busy, so I appreciate you taking the time to consider my request.

You'll note that for the second option the sender acknowledged the recipient's workload and thanked him for considering the email. If you're a newbie reaching out to someone who's extremely accomplished, it's always wise to be as polite and gracious as possible.

Reconnecting with Old Contacts

Some people are great at regularly keeping tabs on all of their contacts, but most of us mere mortals are not. That said, getting back in touch with someone after a long hiatus doesn't have to be awkward. The key here is to do your homework and be human, by which I mean be kind, be curious, and be generous. Google the person to see what he or she has been up to lately, give them a highlight or two about what you've been doing, and ask how they're doing or share an article or idea that might interest them. Here's an example of how you might reach out to set up a coffee meeting.

Hi Fred—It's been too long since we talked. I saw that you just started working at a new startup. Congrats! How's it going so far? Are you enjoying the work?

I've been heads-down the past few months working on a new screenplay and am finally coming up for air. Would you be game to get a coffee sometime in the next few weeks and catch up?

If you don't need to set up a get-together, sharing articles, books, or ideas is a great way to quickly reconnect with someone. For example,

> *Hi Natalie—How's life on the West Coast? I was thinking about our discussions regarding the future of work recently as I was reading Tyler Cowan's book* Average Is Over. *Definitely recommended reading. You can check out* WSJ*'s review here: [link]*

What you want to avoid is reconnecting with people only when you need something from them. If you're getting back in touch just to get something, your contact will know, and it will likely sour the relationship. Try to make a regular habit of connecting to share something positive, whether it's an article link as above, a shout-out for some good press your contact got, or a quick message on social media. Then when you truly need to ask for something, you won't seem slimy.

Writing a Thank You Email

We've talked a lot about asking in this book. The oft-forgotten corollary to asking is, of course, saying thank you. Did someone make an introduction that helped you out in your career? Did someone work with you on a project that really took off? Did someone do you a favor when you were in a pinch? Send them a thank you note and increase the good vibes in their inbox. It makes people feel warm and fuzzy inside to know they have helped someone. And as we discussed earlier, it also makes them more likely to help you or someone else again next time. Here's one example.

> *Hi Carla—Thank you so much for taking the time to review my bio and offer detailed feedback. I just posted the revised version on my website, and I feel much more confident pitching new clients now. I owe you one!*

And here's another.

Hi Mark—We've been getting tons of positive feed-back on the new responsive website you coded for us. Traffic is up 50% on mobile! We could never have done it without you. Much appreciation for all of your great work on the project.

And here's one more.

Hi Sally—How are you doing these days? Remember that conference you recommended I go to last year? Well, I attended and ended up meeting an amazing female entrepreneur who I just founded a new com-pany with! Huge thanks for the tip—you changed the course of my life! :)

People like to know they've done you a good turn. Tell them.

Advanced
Email
Scripts

Pitching Someone You've Never Met

Whether it's trying to land a meeting with a VC, inviting someone to speak at your event, or drumming up new clients, email is the ultimate medium for pitching someone you've never met before. The catch-22? Because everyone is pitching, it's difficult to cut through all the inbox noise and get someone to really pay attention. Thus, every pitch email you write needs to be clear and compelling with zero percent flab.

Although every opportunity is different, there are a few rules of thumb that all good pitch emails follow: they establish what the ask is in the first paragraph, bolster the sender's credibility, demonstrate a well-informed awareness of the recipient's work or company, and they clarify the next step.

Here's a sample email pitching an artist on participating in a book series.

Hi Gail—Lucinda Gray, associate editor at Burnside Press here. I'm assembling a new book of essays and photographs to raise money to battle the spread of malaria. I wanted to see if you might be willing to contribute a photo from your incredible Malawi series?

We did a similar book to raise money to combat tuberculosis last year, and it sold 50,000 copies and raised over a million dollars to fund treatment.

Because we give away 90% of the book proceeds, we can only offer you a small licensing fee of $500. That said, we anticipate that the book will reach a massive audience.

If you're interested, I'd love to do a quick 5-min phone call to share details on participating.

Here's another example of how to pitch a brand on sponsoring your event.

Hi Karl—I'm the director of Design Week Austin, which draws 3,000+ creatives to Texas each October to celebrate art and design. My team and our audience are huge fans of BLDR's 3-D printing products, and I wanted to see if you would be interested in discussing sponsorship opportunities?

The theme of this year's design week is 3-D design, so I think it would be a particularly good fit for showcasing your products. Our audience is predominantly designers, makers, and creative influencers from all over the US, and they are always keen to learn about the latest creative technologies. For more details on our event and audience, you can check out this overview deck: [link]

I would love the chance to speak with you about how we might partner up and create something really special for BLDR at our event. Looking forward to hearing from you.

You can find more snippets from pitch emails on pages 104–106. No matter what you're pitching, craft your email with a focus on emphasizing the benefits for the other person rather than the benefits for you. Imagine that you're reading the email you wrote, strapped for time or strapped for money—would you reply?

Negotiating a Fee with Someone Else

There is little profit in delaying discussions of money. Even so, many people prefer to leave discussion of a fee out of their initial pitch emails, not because they're being strategic but because they prefer to put off awkward conversations about money until the last possible minute. This is a mistake. Generally speaking, if money is involved in a proposal, it should be discussed as soon as possible. Because many of us struggle with this task, a few pointers on how to bring money into the conversation with grace:

Mention the fee up front. Integrating the fee into your pitch from the start shows respect for the recipient by giving them all the information they need to make a decision about the opportunity you're proposing. It also challenges you to frame the fee as a compelling aspect of your overall pitch.

The exception to this rule is when you are the seller rather than the buyer of the services being pitched, and the fee is very large. For example, if you're pitching a sponsor on your event, you don't want to come off like, *Hi, nice to meet you. Give me $50,000.* In instances like this you might include proposed fees for sponsorship levels in a downloadable deck that you link to from the pitch email. This allows you to set expectations around fees early on without seeming aggressive or presumptuous.

Be fair, and don't lowball. Some people feel like low-balling is a necessary part of the negotiation process. In fact, most veteran negotiators will tell you that it's better to propose a fair rate from the get-go if you want the process to go smoothly and remain amicable. Look at the standard rates for the work you're proposing and offer a fee you think is reasonable.

Clarify why the fee is low if necessary. Sometimes you just have a crappy budget and can only offer a fee that you know is rather low. In this case acknowledge that the fee is low and try to offer some convincing reasons why the project is still worth the recipient's time. Maybe it offers massive exposure, or maybe it's for a great nonprofit cause. Regardless, don't just cross your fingers and hope they don't notice—address the issue head on.

Don't use relative terms like "small" or "large" without attaching a number. If you write that there's a "small fee" in your initial email but don't clarify what it is, you invite the recipient to mentally fill in the blank with a number. But "small" is a relative term. You might be thinking $1,000, while the recipient is thinking $5,000. Then, when you reveal the small fee later, the person you've been pitching could be disappointed or, worse, offended. That's why it's best to anchor their expectations to a real number immediately.

Let's say you're launching a new product and need to hire a videographer to create a short video about it. You might want to approach them like this:

Hi Matt—Mike, head of Worth Designs here. Nice to meet you. I'm a huge fan of your product demo work— really gorgeous stuff.

I'm about to launch a new iPhone accessory that allows you to mount your phone securely on your bicycle. I need to create a 60–90 second promo video for

it in the next month, and I wanted to see if you would
be interested in the project?

We're just getting started as a business, so I am
working on a relatively tight budget for the launch. I
worked the numbers, and I can offer you a $3,500 flat
fee for the project. I can also tell you we're generally
very easy to work with. ;)

We'd love to collaborate with you on this. Looking
forward to hearing from you.

(You can find another example of wrapping a fee into a
pitch in the previous essay on pages 181–182.)

Talking about money doesn't have to be adversarial. In
fact, I've found that honesty, clarity, and fairness are significantly better assets in a successful negotiation than
aggression and trickery. A true professional always ap-
preciates straight-forwardness.

Negotiating a Fee for Yourself

Talented individuals undersell their skills and services every day because they can't stomach a frank discussion about money. Although there's no denying that negotiation can be uncomfortable, the payoff for tolerating it can be huge. A mere 15 to 30 minutes of discomfort now will typically increase your wages for years into the future. If you intend to make your livelihood by getting paid to do meaningful creative work, you literally cannot afford to ignore the importance of becoming your own best financial advocate.

Let's say you're a web developer, and a client has gotten in touch about coding a new WordPress site. Because you don't want to waste time if they can't afford your services, it's time to broach the subject of money. Here's how you could do it.

Hi Don—Thanks for reaching out about your new project. I would love to work with you on the website, and I have room in my schedule, as I'm just wrapping up a big project. So the timing is perfect.

For WordPress web development, my usual rate is $150/hour. But for a large project of this type, I can base my estimate on a discounted rate of $100/hour. I anticipate the project will take 3 weeks, so that would be $16,000 for the full project. That includes me setting up a testing environment for building and debugging the site and helping you migrate the new site over to your domain for launch.

If this rate works for you, I can put a formal contract together and we can schedule a project kickoff call in the next 1-2 weeks. Excited to get this project underway!

Now, let's break down what's good about this email. First of all, the web developer sounds enthusiastic, communicating that she is excited about the job being proposed. Then, she shares details about her schedule, indicating that although it's typically quite busy, now happens to be a good time. Rather than seeming desperate for work, she makes it clear her skills are in demand. When she shares her rate, she deliberately frames it as a deal for the client, indicating that she's already coming down in price. This makes it easier for the client to see the rate positively and for the web developer not to deviate too much from her already low rate if the client pushes back on her. Finally, she clarifies what the next steps are and reemphasizes her enthusiasm for the project. This gives a momentum to the conversation, implying she's ready to go as soon as the client approves the rate.

You'll also note that she did not say, *Let me know if this rate is okay for you?* This type of phrasing is practically begging for further negotiation and should be avoided. Instead, the web developer uses language that reinforces the conviction that her rate proposal is fair, and there's no reason why the client shouldn't just approve it and get the project underway.

Even if you secretly feel uncomfortable and hesitant, strive to appear confident, convincing, and professional when you negotiate fees. The upside of email is that no one can see what's going on behind the scenes, so they'll never know you agonized over every word in the draft. Gradually you'll become more comfortable with the process as you see people accept your "bold" pricing proposals without batting an eyelid.

Getting Clients to Pay You

Clients can't seem to stop emailing you when they need assets, edits, and updates on projects. Yet when the project wraps and you want to get paid, an uncanny email silence often ensues. When the client needed things from you, the emails flowed like water. Now that you need something, the well runs dry. How to deal with this aggravating situation?

The best way to avoid having to beg your clients for money is to anticipate this unsavory situation—and plan to avoid it—long before it arrives. That means having an honest and professional conversation about money upfront with all your clients. These are the key issues you should address:

Set the terms for payment before the project starts. What is your fee? On what schedule will it be paid? For example, you might require 50 percent on project start and 50 percent on completion. How will it be paid (e.g., check, wire transfer, PayPal, etc.)? The client will be extremely motivated to work out these details if you clarify that they must be firmed up *before the project starts*. If you wait until after the project starts or, worse, when it's finished, the client is significantly less invested.

An example of how you can broach the subject of payment after you agree on a fee:

Hi Tim—Excited to be collaborating on this project! Before we get started I want to make sure we're on the same page about fees and payment terms. (Boring, I know, but it helps me keep the lights on!)

My standard billing terms are a 50% deposit on project start and then the remaining 50% due upon project completion after I send you final files and they are approved. Because we're in different countries, PayPal is probably the easiest payment system for us to use. Does that work for you?

If you can confirm, I'll pop these details into a brief contract and shoot it over to you for electronic signature. Then we can get going on the fun stuff!

Have the client to sign a contract. Once you've agreed on the terms, put them in writing and have the client sign a contract. Then if things go south, you have legal protection. But more importantly you have conveyed that you have a professional attitude toward managing your projects and getting paid. When you share the agreement with your client, bear in mind that no one is going to fax you back a paper contract in this day and age. There are a variety of online services and apps that allow you to source basic contract templates, tailor them to your specific needs, and send the final document for electronic signature. For my recommendations on specific services, see the Resources section on page 213.

Invoice the client promptly. Much to my chagrin, many of the freelancers I've hired over the years were terrible about invoicing in a timely manner. The longer you wait to bill after the project is complete, the more distance the client feels from owing you anything. What's more, people like to get rid of money when they've budgeted for it, not months later. All of which means: Leverage the natural momentum of the project and bill immediately upon completion. (And if you're doing a deposit to start the project, do not start the project until the deposit is received.) An example of a follow-up email to invoice a client:

> *Hi Tim—Glad the final files looked good! It's been a real pleasure to work with you guys on this project.*
>
> *Attached is my invoice for the 50% balance due on project completion. I've included my email address on the invoice so you can send payment via PayPal as we discussed.*
>
> *Looking forward to working together again in the future!*

Basically, if you seem like you're serious about money, the client is more likely to take the idea of paying you seriously. If it seems like you don't have your shit together and don't really care about getting paid, well, can you really blame the client for not caring either?

Delivering Criticism

Let's start by noting that many types of criticism should not be delivered via email. If your critique relates to someone's personal qualities or performance, that is delicate feedback that you will want to deliver in person. (For example, telling an intern that he didn't handle himself well in a pitch meeting, confronting a colleague about why she missed deadline, or asking your boss not to cut you off when you're speaking to clients.) If the criticism relates to work that someone has created, email discussions usually work fine as long as they're handled with care.

When delivering criticism, the first step is to be kind. No one likes a blast of unmitigated negativity in her inbox. Try to start your email by appreciating some aspect of the work they've done, then give your recipient clear and constructive feedback that's focused on how you can move forward. Don't just say: *This sucks*. Instead, communicate specifically what's wrong and how the work could be changed for the better. And when you suggest those changes, make sure to use questions—*Could you? Would you?*—so your recipient retains her agency, and it doesn't feel like you're barking orders at her.

Let's say you're working with an illustrator on some artwork for an annual report. She's just delivered the first batch of sketches, and stylistically they're not quite what you were hoping for.

Hi Tara—Thanks for turning these around so quickly! It's really helpful to see some early sketches of your illustration ideas.

While these sketches are very beautiful, I feel like the aesthetic is prettier and more ornate than what we're going for. Could we do another batch of preliminary sketches that focus on taking a cleaner, more minimal approach?

I've attached a few sample images from other illustrators below to give you a sense of the minimal look and feel I'm talking about.

Another tip for giving criticism is to use the word "yet" whenever possible. Note the difference between saying:

These designs are not where I want them to be. Versus saying: *These designs are not where I want them to be yet.* By adding that one tiny word you put the recipient on a timeline of learning and achievement rather than shutting them down cold.[27]

Whatever type of critique you're offering, remember that your recipient is a human who's trying her best, just like you are a human who's trying your best. Talk to each other as such and direct any critiques at the work, not the person, and you'll be fine.

Responding to Angry Customers

Angry customers can be quite unpleasant. That said, as soon as they receive a response from a reasonable person who's willing to work with them, they typically change their tune and behave much better. (Most people are only assholes when they think they're shouting into the void.) That's why it's important to keep a cool head and know that the tide will change when you're dealing with someone who's upset.

Let's say you run a conference and get an angry email that sounds like this:

I tried to sign up for the sketching workshop as soon as registration opened today, but I got rejected because it was already full. I paid $1,000 to attend your conference, and now you're telling me I can't go to the workshop I want to attend?! This is bullshit.

A good response might be:

Hi James—I understand your disappointment. The workshops book up fast because they each have a

50-person limit, as our goal is to create an intimate environment. Unfortunately, because we have over 800 attendees, we can't give everyone their first choice and still keep the class sizes small.

But here's what I'm going to do for you: I made a waitlist for the sketching class and you're #1 on it. We typically have a few cancellations leading up to the event, so I expect we'll be able to move you into that workshop very soon. I'll notify you the moment I have an update. Thanks for your patience.

Even if they're being rude, it's never—*never*—productive to argue with a customer. And usually they have a legitimate reason for being upset. Put yourself in the customer's position and start by empathizing with them. If there's a good explanation for the error they're experiencing, share it with them—briefly. If there's been a real screw-up, apologize briefly. Then—and this should be the key focus of the email—tell them how you're going to remedy the situation.

Rejecting an Application or Pitch

Rejection is like ripping off a Band-Aid—it's best not to prolong the process. When you're turning away a job applicant or declining a pitch, don't dilly-dally or over-explain. You needn't share your reasons for the rejection unless you have the time and are strongly convinced the recipient desires such constructive criticism. For the most part, explanations only open the door for further discussion. (Think of it like trying to give your reasons for breaking up with someone. Does it help? Nope. In fact, it usually just prolongs the agony and makes everyone feel worse.) Here's an example of how you can say no to a job applicant.

Hi there—Thanks for applying for our community manager position. We reviewed your application and feel that your experience isn't the right fit for this job.

We do appreciate your interest in the company and wish you the best of luck with your future endeavors.

This is an example of how you can decline a pitch:

Hi Tim—Thanks for pitching us this feature on spec. I've reviewed it, and I don't think it's the right fit for our publication.

However, sometimes you want to decline a specific pitch but encourage further efforts. If that's the case, tell them exactly why their pitch was off and what they need to fix for next time, such as:

Hi Tim—Thanks for pitching us this feature on spec. Although it's well written, I don't think it's the right fit for our publication. We're more focused on articles that provide the reader with actionable advice rather than in-depth profiles that showcase someone's lifestyle. I'd be happy to receive another pitch from you in the future, but you might want to familiarize yourself with the style of our most popular posts and submit something that hits our sweet spot.

If you do not want to encourage further pitches or applications, do not say anything that will give the recipient the impression that the door is still open. Such clarity and finality can feel cruel, but adding additional language to "soften the blow" only serves to create false hope. Say your piece and sign off.

Declining an Introduction or Contact Request

Sometimes people overreach. They might ask you for an introduction you don't think is warranted or to share contact info for a client that it took you years to land. This can create a sticky situation: you don't necessarily want to be rude, but at the same time you don't feel comfortable trading on your credibility or hard work for this person. To decline an introduction request, you might say,

Hi Claire—I'd love to help you out, but my relationship with [insert contact's name] is still fairly new, so I don't really feel comfortable making introductions at this juncture.

Or to deflect a request for a client's contact info you could write,

Hi Dan—I wish I could help you out, but all contact information for our clients is considered proprietary company information. Unfortunately I'm not at liberty to share it with competitors.

Every time you make an introduction, you're essentially endorsing that person as you make the connection. If you're not comfortable with leveraging your credibility for someone or it's not the right moment to do so, it's fine to politely decline the request. As we've discussed already, just because someone asked doesn't mean they expect a yes.

Creating an Auto-Responder
to Handle Email Overload

Once you reach a certain level of renown, it can become impossible to respond to every single email you receive. Unfortunately the outside world—that is, everyone who is emailing you—won't know about this situation unless you tell them. One way to deal with this problem is to set up an email auto-responder to set expectations. Here's an example of a mission-centric auto-responder.

Hi there—This is an auto-response because I now receive more email than one human can reasonably respond to.

As a result, I am only replying to emails that align with my mission of helping people find more meaning and creativity in their daily work.

I will do my best to get to your email, but it may not be possible. Thank you for understanding.

I also like the friendly auto-responder that Tina Roth Eisenberg, founder of Tattly and CreativeMornings, uses:

> *Hi there—This auto-responder is an attempt in setting expectations right. I get too much email and can't keep up. My inbox has become my primary source of guilt.*
>
> *I promise I will try my best to get back to you as soon as I can. If your email is important, and you don't hear back from me, try tweeting to me: @swissmiss! Thank you for understanding!*

If you don't want to use an auto-responder but are still overwhelmed, another option is to explain the situation on your website's contact page. This approach offers the added bonus of setting expectations *before* someone emails you. Writer Cal Newport has a great message on his contact page:

> *A consequence of my commitment to deep work and fixed-schedule productivity is that I'm purposefully*

hard to reach. I don't have a general-use e-mail address, and I don't use any social media. The limited time I can put aside for writing I like to dedicate fully to writing the best possible content.

One of the advantages of running a blog, however, is that it exposes you to interesting opportunities. With this in mind, if you want to interview me or have an offer, opportunity, or introduction that might make my life more interesting, e-mail me at interesting@ calnewport.com. For the reasons stated above, I'll only respond to those proposals that are a good match for my schedule and interests.

Artist and author Austin Kleon makes a point of setting clear email expectations on his contact page as well:

Please note: I get so much email that it's impossible for me to respond to most of it! (If I did, I'd have no time to actually, you know, make anything.) It's nice to hear from readers and fans, and I read everything, but I just can't keep up with it all. Forgive me in advance.

Kleon and Newport both offer a variety of links below the messages I've quoted to filter curious people to the right place from the get-go—their speaking agents' emails for inquiries about talks, their literary agents' emails for inquiries about rights, and so forth.

The more proactive you are about filtering people to the right contact or resource *before* they email you and the more clear you are about setting expectations once someone does email you, the better off you'll be. As they like to say in sports: the best defense is a great offense.

Apps, Extensions, and Other Email Resources

Please note that recommendations and URLs below were good at the time of print, but technology is a fickle thing. So apps may well become outmoded and websites may disappear. If one of my recommendations is no longer available, you can likely Google something similar. Be resourceful!

Gmail extensions that will superpower your productivity. If you don't have it already, download Inbox Pause (inboxpause.com) immediately; this extension allows you to pause your incoming mail so you're not distracted by incoming messages while you're dealing with the mail you already have. If you need to power through your email on an airplane or while you're in some other type of Wifi blackhole, get Gmail Offline (bit.ly/1oJ9lZL), which allows you to access your mail without wireless and then batch send it when you're back online. Lastly, there's a Chrome smart skin called Sortd (sortd.com) that allows you sort and view your Gmail inbox in customized columns such as To Do, Followup, and Deals.

Calendar apps that play well with email. As mentioned earlier in this book, I strongly recommend pulling your calendar app out of email so you don't get sucked into your inbox every time you need to check your schedule. To get you jumpstarted, here are a few recommended mobile calendar apps, most of which work with iCloud, Google Exchange, and Outlook Exchange. For Mac, my personal picks are Fantastical 2 (flexibits.com/fantastical), TinyCal (www.plumamazing/mac/tinycal), and Calendars 5 (readdle.com/calendars5). For Android, the crowd favorites are DigiCal (digibites.nl), SolCalendar (sol.daum .net/calendar), and CloudCal (pselis.com).

Systems for filing your emails in a more organized manner. If you're the type of person who feels peace of mind when everything is in its right place, you might want to implement a folder system to optimize how you sort, handle, and track your emails. But because we all have different workflow preferences and habits, there's no one-size-fits-all folder structure that's guaranteed to work for everyone. A few helpful examples of different approaches to foldering: creatives might enjoy illustrator Jessica Hische's system (http://bit.ly/1wUk9F7), business

types usually dig David Allen's folder setup (http://bit
.ly/1oo9VjM), and minimalists might vibe with Merlin
Mann's approach (http://bit.ly/1TeEujo).

**Apps for sourcing, sending, and signing contracts via
email.** Shake (shakelaw.com) and Docracy (docracy.com)
are both great resources for sourcing and managing contracts. Shake is well designed and speedy to use, featuring
contracts for startup entrepreneurs, designers, filmmak-
ers, musicians, and more. It's free for individual use and
paid for business use. Docracy is a free, open-source library of legal documents for founders, photographers, designers, freelancers, and many more. It also allows you to
negotiate the contract's terms and track changes with
multiple parties before you sign an agreement.

Sneaky tools for unsubscribing from inbox clutter.
Unroll.me is an amazing tool for cleaning up your inbox
on your desktop or iOS device. It scans your inbox for
subscription emails and then allows you to either unsubscribe from those emails en masse or have them rolled
into one single daily digest email. Now you get one email
a day instead of ten or twenty. But the true email pro has

another trick up her sleeve: Email on Deck (emailondeck. com), a service that provides free temporary email addresses that look real but are not. This is ideal for when you need to submit an email address to get access to something but you don't actually want to subscribe to yet another email newsletter.

Acknowledgments

It would never have occurred to me to write this book without the enthusiastic encouragement of my former colleague Sean Blanda and the remarks of illustrator Wendy MacNaughton, whose first words to me when we met in person were, "You are such a great emailer!" Had she chosen to lead instead with a comment about my fabulous hair who knows if this book would have come to pass.

My editor at PublicAffairs, Colleen Lawrie, deserves much gratitude for being a wonderful cheerleader for this project, giving me invaluable input on how to refine this manuscript, responding with admirable swiftness to my anxiety-ridden emails about what to title the book, and always wording her messages to me with infinite tact and encouragement. I must also thank my lovely agent Meg Thompson for connecting me with PublicAffairs as well as for her boundless enthusiasm and unfailing support in thinking that a little ol' book about email could actually be successful.

I want to extend enormous appreciation to my illustrator, José Cardoso (alias: Tomba Lobos), for the incredible artwork featured throughout this book. Despite the challenges of having to communicate from Portland, Oregon, to Porto, Portugal, to get the illustrations done, working with José was one of my favorite creative collaborations ever. This book would be significantly less engaging without his inspired contributions.

I have to thank Sean Blanda (again) and Brock Labrenz for being my first readers and giving me the feedback that made this manuscript ever so much better in the early stages. A bit later on, Morgwn Rimel, Georgia Frances King, Natalie Silverstein, Ayse Birsel, Mark McGuinness, and Matias Corea all took time out of their busy lives to read drafts, assess designs, and provide crucial input and encouragement. You would think that such a tiny little book would pop out fully formed, but in fact it demanded numerous drafts and ruthless editing. (Rather like good email.)

I've had much help in shaping the thoughts contained in this book as well. Behavioral economist Dan Ariely shared the work of B.F. Skinner and how it related to email in an interview for another book I edited called *Manage Your Day-to-Day*. Leadership adviser Scott McDowell introduced me to Daniel Goleman's research on the negativity bias, which explained so many emails gone wrong.

Writer Oliver Burkeman brought the life-changing "askers vs guessers" distinction to my attention in an article for *The Guardian*. Behance co-founder and friend Scott Belsky convinced me of the underrated importance of making progress visible in the digital era. Deep thinker Linda Stone introduced me to the concept of "continuous partial attention." Designer James Victore encouraged me to be a "warrior not a worrier." And my Twitter comrade Bernie Michalik showed me the importance of thinking about communication in terms of people that matter.

Thank you to my wonderful girlfriend, Nissa, for supporting me and putting up with an occasionally very ornery human during the writing of this book. And much love to my parents and my brother for always supporting my creative endeavors and pushing me to accomplish more.

Finally, thanks to you, dear reader, for making it this far! If you're feeling just a little bit less despair about your email, I think my work here is done.

Notes

1. Chimamanda Ngozi Adichie, *Americanah* (New York: Anchor Books, 2013), 375.

2. Ernest Becker, *The Denial of Death* (New York: Free Press Paperbacks, 1997), xviii.

3. Jason Fried, "What Are Questions?" *Signal v. Noise*, August 2, 2012, https://signalvnoise.com/posts/3225-what-are-questions.

4. Gloria Mark, Shamsi Iqbal, Mary Czerwinski, and Paul Johns, "Focused, Aroused, but So Distractible: A Temporal Perspective on Multitasking and Communications," Proceedings of 18th ACM Conference, Computer Supported Cooperative Work and Social Computing (CSCW 2015), New York, ACM Digital Library.

    Michael Chui and McKinsey Global Institute, *The Social Economy: Unlocking Value and Productivity Through Social Technologies* (New York: McKinsey & Company, July 2012).

    Kostadin Kushlev and Elizabeth W. Dunn, "Checking Email Less Frequently Reduces Stress," *Computers in Human Behavior* 43 (February 2015): 220–228.

5. Dan Ariely, "Understanding Our Compulsions," in *Manage Your Day-to-Day: Build Your Routine, Find Your Focus, and*

Sharpen Your Creative Mind, ed. Jocelyn K. Glei (Las Vegas: Amazon, 2013), 89–94.

6. Francesca Gino and Bradley Staats, "Your Desire to Get Things Done Can Undermine Your Effectiveness," *Harvard Business Review*, March 22, 2016, https://hbr.org/2016/03/your-desire-to-get-things-done-can-undermine-your-effectiveness.

    Tiage Zhang, "The Power of the Progress Bar," Kissmetrics, https://blog.kissmetrics.com/the-progress-bar.

7. Teresa Amabile and Steven J. Kramer, "The Power of Small Wins," *Harvard Business Review*, May 2011, https://hbr.org/2011/05/the-power-of-small-wins.

8. Daniel Goleman, "The Danger of Email," LinkedIn Pulse, February 22, 2013, www.linkedin.com/pulse/20130222162001-117825785-the-danger-of-email.

9. "Reciprocity (social psychology)," Wikipedia, https://en.wikipedia.org/wiki/Reciprocity_(social_psychology).

10. Alix Spiegel, "Give and Take: How the Rule of Reciprocation Binds Us," *Morning Edition*, NPR, November 26, 2012, www.npr.org/sections/health-shots/2012/11/26/165570502/give-and-take-how-the-rule-of-reciprocation-binds-us.

11. Tangerine, January 16, 2007, comment on Jeffxl, "What's the Middle Ground Between 'F.U!' and 'Welcome!'?" Ask Meta-Filter, January 16, 2007, http://ask.metafilter.com/55153/Whats-the-middle-ground-between-FU-and-Welcome#830421.

Oliver Burkeman, "Are You an Asker or a Guesser?" *Guardian*, May 7, 2010, www.theguardian.com/lifeandstyle/2010/may/08/change-life-asker-guesser.

12. Lauren Schwartzberg, "How Tavi Gevinson Stays Productive," *Fast Company*, June 15, 2015, www.fastcompany.com/3046799/most-creative-people/how-tavi-gevinson-stays-productive.

13. Jordie van Rinj, "The Ultimate Mobile Email Statistics Overview," emailmonday, September 2015, www.emailmonday.com/mobile-email-usage-statistics.

14. Gloria Mark, Shamsi Iqbal, Mary Czerwinski, Paul Johns, and Akane Sano, "Email Duration, Batching and Self-Interruption: Patterns of Email Use on Productivity and Stress," *Proceedings of the 2016 CHI Conference on Human Factors in Computing Systems*, 1717–1728 (New York: ACM Press, 2015).

Kushlev and Dunn, "Checking Email Less Frequently Reduces Stress."

15. A. Bucciol, D. Houser, and M. Piovesan. "Temptation at Work," Harvard Business School Research Paper, no. 11–090, 2011, http://www.hbs.edu/faculty/Publication%20Files/11-090.pdf.

16. Clive Thompson, "Meet the Life Hackers," *New York Times Magazine*, October 16, 2005, www.nytimes.com/2005/10/16/magazine/meet-the-life-hackers.html?_r=1.

17. Gloria Mark, Victor M. Gonzalez, and Justin Harris, "No Task Left Behind?: Examining the Nature of Fragmented Work," in *Proceeding of the SIGCHI Conference on Human Factors in Computing Systems*, 321–330 (Portland, OR: ACM Press, 2005).

18. Mark et al., "Email Duration, Batching and Self-Interruption."

19. Benjamin V. Hanrahan and Manuel A. Pérez-Quiñones, "Lost in Email: Pulling Users Down a Path of Interaction," in *Proceedings of the 33rd Annual ACM Conference on Human Factors in Computing Systems*, 3981–3984 (CHI '15) (New York: ACM Press, 2015).

20. Daniel Pink, "How to Pitch Better: The Email Pitch," DanPink.com, www.danpink.com/2013/06/how-to-pitch-better-the-email-pitch.

21. Linda Stone, "Continuous Partial Attention?" Lindastone. net, https://lindastone.net/qa/continuous-partial-attention.

22. Van Rinj, "Mobile Email Statistics Overview."

23. Adam M. Grant and Francesca Gina, "A Little Thanks Goes a Long Way: Explaining Why Gratitude Expressions Motivate Prosocial Behavior," *Journal of Personality and Social Psychology* 98, no. 6 (June 2010): 946–955.

24. E. B. White, *Here Is New York* (New York: Little Book Room, 1999), 25.

25. Shea Bennett, "28% of Time Spent Online Is Social Networking," *Adweek*, January 27, 2015, www.adweek.com/social-times/time-spent-online/613474.

26. Lewis Hyde, *The Gift: Creativity and the Artist in the Modern World* (New York: Vintage Books, 2007), 65.

27. Carol Dweck, "The Power of Believing That You Can Improve," TEDxNorrkoping, November 2014, www.ted.com /talks/carol_dweck_the_power_of_believing_that_you _can_improve/transcript?language=en.